Voices
and Visions

SAM KEEN

1817

Harper & Row, Publishers
New York, Evanston, San Francisco, London

T. George Harris

Robert Poteete.

Both editors and friends.

VOICES AND VISIONS Copyright©1970, 1971, 1972, 1973, 1974 by Ziff-Davis Publishing Company.Introduction Copyright©1974 by Sam Keen. All rights reserved. Printed in the United States of America. No part of this book may be used or reproduced in any manner whatsoever without written permission except in the case of brief quotations embodied in critical articles and reviews. For information address Harper & Row, Publishers, Inc., 10 East 53rd Street, New York, N.Y. 10022. Published simultaneously in Canada by Fitzhenry & Whiteside Limited, Toronto.

FIRST EDITION

Designed by C. Linda Dingler

Library of Congress Cataloging in Publication Data

Keen, Sam.
  Voices and visions.

  1. Consciousness. 2. Visions. I. Title.
BF311.K36   154   74–4624
ISBN 0–06–064260–2

Enjoyed
being with
you &
savoring
your
spirit

Sam Keen

Voices and Visions

Also by Sam Keen

GABRIEL MARCEL

APOLOGY FOR WONDER

TO A DANCING GOD

TELLING YOUR STORY (with Anne Valley Fox)

Contents

Introduction

The editors of *Psychology Today* recently received the following letter:

Dear People,

I have a suggestion for an article. How about getting ol' Sam Keen to write some sort of essay on what he's learned from some of the truly interesting people he's interviewed. Actually, I don't care at all to hear about that. I want to know if he has had any truly enlightening experiences. I would think after talking to Castaneda, Lilly, and Ichazo one would have to alter one's lifestyle and thought patterns. Has he succeeded in reaching any higher levels of awareness? If so, I would love to read about them. He has a very distinctive characteristic in his writings. He quotes, he has the factual knowledge, but the question is does it touch his heart, does he feel this knowledge or has he experienced it? That's the important thing. As one who does *not* feel it, I'd like to hear how someone gets beyond the read and quote state to the experience stage.

Oh well,
Elizabeth Louise Foxwell

Dear Elizabeth Foxwell,

In any conversation the person who asks the questions shapes the dialogue. It's good that you want to know about the questioner. My life has been a search. For as long as I can remember I have been asking: What does it mean to be a person? and What is happening in the twentieth century? I talked to each one of these thinkers because I thought I had something to learn. Consequently I have been changed by listening. These formal conversations

3

are the tip of an iceberg. Beneath the surface of the philosophical questions lie the massive fact and feeling of my personal life and the currents of the modern world which has been my home. There is not space and time enough to share my story with you in detail. But I would like to tell enough to show some of the connections between my head and my heart. Here is your essay about what it means to me.

Cordially,
Sam Keen

It takes a hundred tellings and more to begin to capture the themes that make up a single autobiography. In *To a Dancing God* I told of growing up in small Southern towns, of my struggle to break free of fundamentalism, of the intellectual excitement of Harvard, of the first steps in discovering a way of life that was more passionate than anything I had known as a young professor. In a future book I want to write about the years after 1969 when I moved west and became engulfed in the California madness. That story includes love and sex, marriage and divorce, drugs and politics, and what little I know of touching and caring for the sacredness of fleeting things.

One chapter in my autobiography would have to be called: "Meetings With Famous Men." I ceased to be a child when I learned to listen to Kierkegaard, Hegel, Nietzsche, and Freud. And during my time at Harvard I learned from talking with Paul Tillich, Gabriel Marcel, and Howard Thurman. When I joined the staff of *Psychology Today*, I merely continued formally and in print doing what I had been doing privately for years—asking questions, posing problems, talking, listening. The conversations which make up this book are no less a part of my story than the famous rubber-gun wars of Maryville, Tennessee or my love affair in Istanbul.

For me the 1970's began with an explosion. I was approaching the mythical year forty. And true to the archetype, I left my secure home and went wandering. After seventeen years of marriage I followed a lovely gypsy girl deep into the forest and before I knew it I was lost. The We that had contained my I came apart. Divorce. And when my elusive gypsy finally slipped beyond my reach, the loneliness I had run from for a lifetime settled upon me. And the face of death filled the empty nights. (One is one and all alone and evermore shall be so.) In the process of divorce and relocation, I dropped out of academic life and professorial tweeds and became a freelance writer, lecturer, and group leader. Then came the barren apartments, and the slow effort to put down roots in a new town and learn how to father my absent children. So much for hard facts. Anyone who wishes to read between the lines can hear the story of the changes which have gradually softened my mind and loosened a wild wind in my imagination.

During this period of transition, two questions have been center stage in my mind. The first: What is happening? I was in the middle of interlocking revolutions. In the late sixties and early seventies the New Left was agitating universities and bringing politics back into the streets. The human potential movement was stirring up every conceivable emotion. The psychedelic revolution was opening constipated imaginations and letting all heaven loose and more than a little instant madness. And everywhere advocates of a new consciousness were predicting the dawning of a new age. Supposedly the turmoil was only a birth trauma of the age of Aquarius. Our national neurosis was speeding toward the crisis point where all the old repressive structures would fall away and we would emerge into a participatory democracy, a cosmic consciousness, a post-technological society, a retribalized world, a transformation—the Omega point. After a brief death (the cover of *Time* is a certain obituary) God was shaking himself alive in 1970 and ushering in a new utopia. That, at least, was the hope that fueled the drive of the counterculture.

For me the question What's happening? became linked with a second question: Who am I? If there could be a rebirth of our culture, a consciousness revolution, it seemed reasonable to assume there might also be life after forty. If, on the other hand, no new spirit could surge through history, then my effort to be free of a repressive style of controlling rationality (Words. Explanations. Why? Why? Why? Chatter in the head. Thinking.) seemed less than hopeful. My fate and the fate of my culture seemed linked. Both had been dominated by intellect, calculation, competition and performance, and both were reaching toward a more intuitive, spontaneous, cooperative life style. America and I had lived by the ethic of the Marlboro man, and now we were tired of pseudo-independence, of arrogance, of the old masculine virtues of a tight stomach, a tough heart and a cast iron mind. How were we to understand what was happening to us? Was our identity crisis a sign of decline or metamorphosis? Was our trauma a death rattle or a birth pang? Were we headed down the path to decadence or beginning the hero's journey? Were our minds becoming uncorseted and wallowing in the occult, or were we discovering the poetry of the spirit? These were the questions I went about asking some of the people I had reason to think had wisdom to share.

I began with Norman O. Brown. I had discovered his books *(Life Against Death* and *Love's Body)* in my discarnate years as a professor. When he spoke of the obsession to labor and produce, and of the body which was drained of eros and controlled by the head (capitalism) I recognized myself. For the first time I had a psychological and sociological map which allowed me to understand the nature of my alienation. Being a Western man, I knew I had inherited a cultural tradition which drove a wedge between mind and body, self and world. And when Brown spoke about a reunion which involved the resurrection of the body and the creation of a Dionysian consciousness, I saw a vision of wholeness, which I explored in *Apology for Wonder* (New York: Harper & Row, 1969). But Brown worried me. I knew enough about the divine madness of Dionysus from my experience with LSD to appreciate how much anxiety and pain were involved in dissolving the rigid Apollonian structures of the psyche. The sweet madness of Zorba the Greek was lovely, but the rampant anger and confusion which accompanies the loss of boundaries was a more terrifying story. And Brown did not speak about the deadly traps of the unconscious in which every psychonaut becomes entangled. In *Love's Body,* his organized aphorisms proceeded with poetic precision to make an airtight argument against airtight systems. The logic with which he worked out a Dionysian vision of the world left me breathless. But what did he mean by a return to body mysticism and the polymorphous perversity of childhood? Was he, like Fritz Perls, advocating that we should lose our minds and come to our senses? Should we become experts in sensory awareness? I wondered if Brown was merely a head-tripper or whether he had changed his style of thinking, feeling, touching, smelling and acting. Was he a prophet like Moses pointing to a promised land in which he was personally unable to dwell?

My chance to talk with Brown came by accident. At a weekend workshop I met T. George Harris, the editor of *Psychology Today*, and he found out about my interest in Brown. *Psychology Today* had commissioned Warren Bennis to do a conversation with Brown, and it had been well started when Bennis' university erupted in political turmoil and he could not finish the conversation. So I was commissioned to complete what Bennis had begun.

Brown's lair, an elegant house on the edge of a golf course, was sedate enough. The grape vines over the terrace and the tea and biscuits served English-style led me to suspect that the Bacchanalian orgies thereabouts were in the recesses of Brown's imagination. I asked if he practiced what he preached. Was the Dionysian consciousness he was advocating a mere inner revolution in the structure of the imagination, or did it involve political action and a radical change in life-style? Brown's answer undercut the dualism implied in my question. He insisted on the unity of poetry and politics, imagination and sensation, the inner and outer worlds. "The Eternal Body of Man *is* the imagination." The quotation came from Blake, but it might as easily have come from Raquel Welch, who is rumored to have said, "The mind is the most erogenous zone." The Gordian knot was cut, and I saw a way beyond the alienating dualisms that had held me fast. If there is no separation between mind/body, meaning/fact, imagination/action, vision/revolution, I could not experience more sensuality and warmth by merely emptying my mind of ideas. If eros was to warm my flesh I would have to let it soften the concepts I used to think about the world. My driving mind would have to learn tenderness. Instead of making ideas march goose-step, I would have to allow them to tumble over each other like kittens. But how could I learn to be a player in a society of workers? And how could I bask in delight when my sensitivities also showed me the terror and tragedy of the world? The world might not be saved without a new dream, but no poetry could stop the carnage of Vietnam or drain the abscess of poverty. The transformation of the imagination seemed a necessary but not a sufficient condition for the metamorphosis America and I wanted. We would have to change both the way we thought and the way we lived.

It was obvious that my next conversation should be with Herbert Marcuse. Marcuse had fired the New Left with a vision of a more erotic society in which machines would free us from dehumanizing labor and allow us time to play our way to freedom. His vision was not unlike Brown's, but he advocated direct political and revolutionary means for implementing it. Marcuse substituted Germanic rigor for Brown's Irish mysticism. He charged that Brown was too willing to retreat into poetry and escape from the hard realities of power, class conflict and actual revolution. An erotic imagination may even be a privatistic luxury in a world where power confrontations are necessary to insure justice. For Marcuse, "the real emancipation of man can take place only in a different society after a fundamental change in values and in political and economic structures." The Establishment must be abolished before freedom will arrive. And anything short of a complete revolution—more relaxed attitudes toward sex, the body, and freedom of speech—may be nothing more than repressive desublimation. Halfway measures strengthen the power of the existing Establishment.

Both in reading and talking with Marcuse, I felt the presence of an unyielding mind whose criteria for an acceptable world were so high that nothing actual could pass muster. Either there must be total destruction of The Establishment (an entity not unlike Absolute Spirit in Hegel's system) or a continuation of repression. Talk of total revolution left me feeling impotent, anxious, and desperate. Had America and I to be completely destroyed in apocalyptic fire and be reborn in virginal purity before we could achieve authentic life? If so, there seemed to be no hope. Angry prophets and preachers marshal our guilt, but I suspect they do little to enable us to change. Within the psyche all must be accepted and appreciated before change can take place. My efforts to bully myself toward perfection always ended in frustration. When I observed the resentment that motivated many in the New Left, I suspected the virtues of capitalism would have to be sung before the body politic could purge itself of the vices of exploitation and injustice. A possibly unattainable erotic utopia is hardly a viable replacement for a faulted democracy which has given a majority of its citizens sufficient food and ease to make high cholesterol and diet foods a national obsession. I am aware that my rejection of the way of total revolution probably has a lot to do with being a WASP. If I were on the lower rather than the upper end of the reward scale I might find less to admire in the faulted democracy we have managed to achieve. But even after I compensate for my prejudices, for my ideological blindness, I still cannot envision a modern, complex, industrial society which could be run without a powerful (and therefore elite) government. We might exchange one Establishment for another, as in Cuba and Red China, but the ideal of a society without repression, like the ideal of a completely Dionysian consciousness that would be free from the fear of death and from any fixed boundaries or relationships, was too radical for me to accept. Yet Marcuse and Brown stick in my consciousness like cockleburs. Both remind me, in Western poetry and political philosophy, of the Eastern ideal of the bodhisattva, the man who is on the verge of nirvana and returns to society to labor until all sentient beings can share the bliss of enlightenment. Since every individual consciousness is in constant resonance with the surrounding society, no person can be free so long as any person is enslaved. The same nerve endings with which we feel private passions register our compassion toward the public world beyond the psyche. I and we are one. There is no separation of the body and the body politic. Since personal and public liberation are linked and we live within the tragedies of actual history rather than the ideal utopia, partial liberation is the best we can hope for. The fullest path for the individual is to be responsible for his personal transformation and for some action that may allow society to move in a more just and erotic direction. Evil is always with us; no political program can eliminate it. Every utopian scheme hides a Grand Inquisitor. We make the earth a hell when we insist on turning it into paradise. We do not know how to eliminate evil but, as Camus said, we can feed some of the hungry and heal some of the infirmed.

It was Joseph Campbell's rejection of all utopias and his affection for the faulted beauty of actual existence that first interested me. Perfection is an impossible and destructive ideal. If we are not able to love life with all its infirmities, we end up withholding our affirmation and postponing joy until some future time when we will have molded the world to fit our dreams. For Campbell the true hero is the prodigal son who leaves familiar values, travels into a distant land of alienation and madness, and then has the courage to return to everyday life and affirm its wonder. The hero, like Kierkegaard's Knight of Faith, is marked by the unusual ability to be enthusiastic about the usual. In fact, he is not unlike Joseph Campbell himself, who has maintained a passionate love affair with myths and stories for more than a half a century and has remained a happy intellectual.

I discovered Campbell's *Hero With A Thousand Faces* in my traumatic fortieth year, when I was in chaos. One of the major determinants of the outcome of a psychological crisis is the categories used to interpret it. Was my anxiety, my dislocation, an emotional disorder? A neurosis? A mental disease? If so, it was appropriate that I should be ashamed of my efforts to discover a more passionate way of life, and I should go to a doctor who would cure my mental illness. Fortunately, Campbell gave me a different model for interpreting my dis-ease. He traced the myth of the hero's journey through various cultures and showed that many persons at the midpoint in life must go through a radical transition which involves a descent into the hell of psychological chaos and an eventual rebirth. When I read *Hero* the pain of my rite of passage did not recede, but I lost my shame. I knew from Campbell's map that many before me had made the same journey and that all had passed through dismemberment and ego-death before being miraculously reborn into the wonder of ordinary life.

Campbell also suggested a way to make sense out of the paradoxical relation of the individual and the community. My childhood had been spent as a Yankee in the Deep South. My family moved every year or two, so my brother and I were always outsiders. We were the strange ones, the ready-made enemies of the established gangs, and we spent much of our time playing alone in the woods. Consequently, membership has always been difficult for me, while the virtues and vices of individualism come easily. Campbell states that the hero's journey is only taken by the creative individual who differentiates himself from the crowd and enters the forest at the point where there are no other paths. This celebration of individualism is comfortable to my spirit. In theory, America insures every person the right to create a name for himself (now herself also). The myth of the uniqueness and value of each individual has remained one of our guiding principles. But our individualism has created a society of isolated persons with little sense of community. I exist, but do I belong? I am, but who are my people? The hero's journey joins the individual to the community at the deepest level. Pursue the unique path, insist upon your particularity, tell your own story, and, paradoxically, in the depths of your own individuality you will discover the story of Everyman. Go your own way and you will find the community within yourself. In the heart of your privacy you will discover the same path that was traveled by all the sung and unsung heroes and heroines. Myths continue to speak to us because no autobiography is unique. The most individual life is still impregnated with archetypal patterns. At the heart of our privacy we discover how public we are.

Certain persons seem to crystallize the fears and hopes of a generation. Charles Manson came to represent the evils of the psychedelic revolution, and John Lilly the hope that mysticism could be married to science. We would like our scientists to accumulate hard data and be competent in empirical investigation but to maintain an open stance toward the cosmos. Lilly's work with dolphins, isolation tanks, and altered states of consciousness; and his suggestion that consensus science might need to be supplemented by psychedelic vision, raised the happy possibility that we might not have to sacrifice our religious needs on the altar of science.

Lilly's technique for exploring psychedelic spaces is to establish an observatory within the self from which the most turbulent phenomena can be calmly observed. He encourages us to maintain a genuine objectivity about inner experience. This scientific detachment allows a person to explore any of the kingdoms of the mind. It is within this attitude that science and religion meet. The dispassionate observer of the inner world, the scientist of mental phenomena, is the same as the fair witness self which Eastern religion seeks to cultivate by meditation. Within the mind all thoughts have an equal right to exist. Scientific objectivity is only true democracy or love. No idea or image can be repressed; neither morality nor practicality nor common consensus is required for us to entertain an idea.

John both shocked and intrigued me. He seemed to play with the limits of belief as if there were no danger. His single rule for exploration within the mind was: every belief is a limit to be examined and transcended. The first time I heard this rule my head spun. Every belief? Is there nothing I can hold to? No resting-place free from questions? As a timid explorer of psychedelic spaces I was comfortable with the notion of examining the limits of my old belief systems. I had already shed several worn out skins (old snake in springtime). But I hoped I could work out the bugs in my current beliefs, add a little more elasticity, and come up with a philosophy true enough to last. After half a lifetime of temporary rentals, I wanted to take out a mortgage on my own conceptual home. But Lilly was saying the process of iconoclasm had to continue. I had to remain forever on the road. Come to a limit and transcend it; come to a limit and transcend it; etc. Our only security is in our ability to change. This radical perspective made me look at my desire for security, confront my resistance to change, and realize that I would always remain a philosophical gypsy. (The gypsy I had fallen in love with was within myself!)

Once I faced (a thousand times) my resistance to the unknown, I understood the rightness of John's challenge to remain an explorer, a *homo viator*. But it was not until I floated free in his isolation tank that I fully understood the method of observation. Western man has always had a moral gravity prejudice. As upright animals we spend a good deal of our energy maintaining an erect stance in the world. And the experience of vertical disposition has crept into our way of dealing with inner experience. There are "higher" and "lower," "shallow" and "deep" kinds of experience. Many of our metaphors for the moral life depend upon the image of climbing from base to more elevated levels of being. And spirituality has been nothing more than a special case of upward mobility (getting high). Floating horizontally in an isolation tank releases the body and hence the imagination from the necessity to remain upright and to relate ideas to an exterior world. For the time being there is not world, no interchange. The self is freed from the pressure of context and has an opportunity for a naked confrontation with the workings of the mind. And within the mind there is no better or worse, no good or evil. All possibilities may be entertained. The moral worlds of St. Francis and the Marquis de Sade exist side by side because in our dreams we are saints and killers. In the isolation of the tank—the mind without context—there is no need for judgment or action, and hence no higher or lower states of consciousness. Interior freedom means opening all the doors within the imagination so we can travel into our private hells and heavens. Once this freedom is acquired we can locate any human quality— ecstasy, depression, contentment, anger, boredom, joy—within the confines of our life experience. And once we locate a psychic space we can travel there at will. For instance, I remembered while floating free that I had experienced ecstatic union with the world one summer afternoon when I was about 8 years old. I had been lying on the bank of a stream watching the clouds float toward some unknown beyond, when I dissolved and was at harmony with the world. Now when I want to invite harmony I hold the picture of that moment before my inner eye.

The trick of being a philosophical gypsy is the knowledge that there are endless worlds within the self to be explored. Each time I venture into a strange one I find myself better able to understand the *exterior* world.Freedom to play in the fields of imagination and to perceive the exterior world of "reality" go hand in hand. There may or may not be unicorns in Iowa or spirit guides from distant galaxies. But I can certainly never verify their existence or non-existence if I refuse to entertain the unicorns and angels that romp in my head. Within the realm of the mind there are no limits to what may be entertained, or entertaining.

If John Lilly evoked the archetype of the mystic in the white jacket, Carlos Castaneda conjures up the romantic myth of the wise and noble Indian. A generation of suburban kids who toyed with tipis and beads and whole earth communes made heroes out of Castaneda and his guru don Juan. If analysis and technology offer us nothing better than missiles and moonwalks, perhaps it is time to look for other ways of knowing and acting. It's time for magic and sorcery and exploring separate realities that yield more to spells than electron microscopes. Carlos is to the counterculture what Neil Armstrong is to the establishment: a traveler to a planet outside terrestrial time and space.

The name "Carlos Castaneda" enters most conversations trailing streams of question marks. Is he real? Did he invent don Juan? Is he kidding? Periodically rumors circulate that Carlos has been committed to a mental institution or has committed suicide or has completely disappeared. When Carlos and I were to meet I wondered whether he would appear and if he would be accompanied by a dust devil. I might have saved myself the anxiety had I remembered G.K. Chesterton's words that extraordinary things can only happen to ordinary people. Carlos arrived on the minute by conventional transportation (VW bus) wearing lace-up shoes and accompanied by a delightful woman anthropologist. In our talks he appeared much as he did in his books: both wide-eyed sorcerer's apprentice and analytical college professor. Both as an artist and a person, Carlos is captivating. He weaves a spell with words that leaves his listeners believing anything may be possible. Sorcery is as natural to him as charm. I delighted in his work and his presence and imbibed so much spine-straightening stoicism from his notions of accumulating personal power and becoming a warrior that it was some months before I realized I had many philosophical objections to the view of the world he was advocating.

The magical world of Castaneda fascinates me, but I feel as uncomfortable with its literalism as I did with the fundamentalist Christianity of my early years. The demons and evil spirits I know reside within the complexes of my psyche or my culture: the inferiority complex or the military-industrial complex. Carlos's wanderings in the hills of Mexico seem like those childhood times when I crept into the graveyard on moonlit nights to scare myself with visions of ghosts I knew did not exist. I don't know whether there are witches or spirit entities that inhabit astral dimensions. The evidence for the existence of such beings is gossamer. But I prefer a vision of the world that eliminates as many extraterrestrial entities—witches, ghosts, angels, demons, gods from outer space—as possible. Forests are enchanted enough without elves or hobbits. (Did you ever see a ruby-throated hummingbird?) And there are wonders enough in the ordinary without having to chase miracles. Carlos and don Juan so fill the world with dangerous entities that they have to posit the existence of "allies" to help them combat the malevolent forces. This multiplication of personnel —the demonic and angelic hierarchies—removes human responsibility. The authorities and powers remain exterior, and we have to resort to occult means to control them.

I am also uncomfortable with the metaphors that govern Castaneda's vision—knowledge, power, warfare, and seeing—if they are taken as defining the authentic life. For Carlos, man at best is a warrior who accumulates personal power or a man of knowledge who can stop the world and see. Since the time of Plato there has been an argument among philosophers whether knowledge or love is the higher ideal. Those who favor the way of knowledge believe (with Bacon) that "knowledge is power." Those who believe a person's highest destiny is to become a lover hold that the quest for power must be abandoned as one approaches love. For most of my life I fled from feelings of impotence and sought knowledge and personal power. Now that I have a measure of both, I find the only path with heart is one that makes the heart the ruling organ of the personality. The most dangerous and promising model for me is not the warrior but the lover. I agree with Milton Mayeroff *(On Caring):* "In the sense in which a man can ever be said to be at home in the world, he is at home not through dominating, or explaining, or appreciating, but through caring and being cared for. . . ." The great adventure for me is the risk of moving beyond an adversary relation to other men and women and beyond the subtle metaphysical paranoia which has kept me busy working, doing, trying, accumulating power and personal security. The warrior's way defines the world in terms of danger and conflict and therefore requires the accumulation of armor and power. It is necessary to have the strength to use the sword, but it is more difficult to find the courage to cease using it.

I have Oscar Ichazo to thank for weakening one of my cherished prejudices against Eastern spirituality. As a Western man I have always been shaped by the vision of the world as a battleground between good and evil, a kind of cosmic *High Noon.* Life is agonal, conflictual, and tragic. Consequently, I have suspected Eastern religion offered a retreat from history. I have observed that people who get heavily committed to meditation often lose both their outrage and their compassion. Peace of mind can be gained by withdrawal from the world, by stilling the vortices of the mind. But how much inner peace is appropriate in a world that contains Attica, Vietnam, Johannesburg, Biafra, Pakistan and sub-Sahara Africa? I had been unwilling to consider the meditative way because I thought it allowed an elite class the luxury of pursuing spiritual goals while ignoring the struggle to create a more just social order. Consequently, I had always nurtured a high degree of inner turmoil and agony. My long friendship with Michael Murphy, who had practiced meditation for years, softened my resistance. In my encounters with John Lilly and Oscar, the penny dropped and I realized I did not need to allow a battle to rage within my consciousness in order to be actively concerned about the tragic conflicts of the contemporary world. When I began to meditate I discovered a power of self-transcendence, an ability to rise above and consider from a distance the moods, feelings, and obsessive thoughts which previously had captivated my attention and victimized me. It has been an enormous relief to find an observatory within myself, a calm and kindly perspective, from which I can be nonviolent in dealing with my violence, spontaneous in observing my obsessions, hopeful in the presence of my depression, unafraid of my fears, and comical in the midst of my tragic seriousness. I think each person, like the god Janus, needs two faces. As we face inward we must accept loveliness and evil alike and exert only the gentlest pressure toward change. All that is ugly and distorted within the psyche must be understood and accepted before it can be changed. But the face that looks outward toward the world cannot be so tolerant. When we witness the brutality, injustice, and exploitation that infests the world around us, compassion moves us to act. To understand the political realities which lead to the destruction of our ecology, to the napalming of villages, or to the starvation of millions in sub-Sahara Africa is not enough. We must act to change things.

Oscar Ichazo's method of integrating mysticism and a concern for social change both interests me and makes me very uncomfortable. In the Arica Institute he has created an organization to teach many of the skills that Carlos learned from Don Juan: the techniques of ego reduction, stopping the world, and returning consciousness to the body. But in this case the Mohammed came to the mountain. Oscar came from the desert of Chile to the canyons of New York to make his teachings available in a packaged form that is compatible with the tastes of American disciples. I have known many persons who have been profoundly changed by their participation in Arica. Most are stronger, more confident, and happier. Still I am bothered by the conformity, rigidity, and compulsion that Arica sometimes engenders. It is easy for disciplines and techniques to become ends in themselves, and at times it appears as if Arica has given individual neurotics social sanction for adopting a group neurosis. Private obsession is replaced by public rituals and wall-to-wall spiritual disciplines which leave little place for spontaneity. At its best Arica teaches a wide range of techniques for altering consciousness which have been taken from religious and wisdom schools of East and West. At worst it encourages an antiseptic spiritual obsessionality in which constant working on the state of the soul replaces the risky excitement of ordinary life. I am happy to see the proliferation of Aricas, Esalens, transcendental meditators, Zen academies, and all manner of neo-wisdom schools. It is high time we became interested in the education of the spirit and the integration of body/mind, sexuality/religion, psyche/cosmos. But St. Paul's warning rings true to my third ear: "Works do not produce grace." Discipline, ritual, impeccability, persistent working on one's psyche, like the orthodox demand for correct belief in Jesus, can easily destroy that casual acceptance of the imperfect actuality of life which is the essence of grace. A mixed measure of slapdash carelessness and abandon is necessary to escape the demons of seriousness. (And I'm not kidding.)

I was first attracted to Stanley Keleman by his insistence that vital sexuality and religious mysticism are inseparable. So long as the head governs the body we foster the illusion of control. We believe our words, ideas, and explanations contain reality. In my adult years I have lived in a headstrong manner, full of ideas, oughts, and visions. But the voice of my body has nevertheless remained strong. For as long as I can remember I have wanted the strands in my life to intertwine to form an earthy mysticism. I have been looking for a way to unite the imperatives of thought and feeling, culture and nature. As a child the hymns of the Church spoke the language of the sacred: "God of our lives, through all encircling years, we trust in Thee." But pine woods and meadowlarks and flying squirrels moved me at a level far deeper than any religious words. I knew early that the sacred was to be found in wild places that were not dominated by the will of man. And later, when sex uncoiled from the sleep of latency and ran full length up my spine, I knew even more certainly that we encounter the holy in those untamed places where we tremble in the presence of a mystery.

Norman O. Brown gave me the vision of a body mysticism that would reunite eros with spirit but he offered no practical path. Stan Keleman was a therapist who used bio-energetic techniques to revitalize the body. At selected times in my meanderings when I felt blocked, deadened, or in pain, I worked with Stan. I learned that depression always involved shallow breathing and muscular tension in the chest and shoulders. I learned how to kick and scream and say "no" with the entire force of my body. And after rebellion and anger were released there was sorrow and grief and disappointment lodged in the hollowness of my chest. And weeping. Gradually my body began to soften and yield to increasing pulsations and streamings of warmth. And I noticed a growing communion of head and heart and genitals and world. My work with Stan allowed me to appreciate my peculiar style of embodiment—keen, penetrating, tonic, over-intense—and to begin opening to the softer, more "feminine" sides of myself. It is easier these days to tolerate times of contentment, to accept nourishment, to yield to the sweet and terrible knowledge that floods the mind when the controllers, the judges, and the measurers of the personality are asleep.

The Apollonian side of my personality that loves neat boundaries and sharp definitions and all that is historical and limited found an ally in Earnest Becker. It is good to be able to play in the psychedelic Disneyland of Dionysus, to erase personal history and soar into the cosmic spaces of the imagination, but it is a relief to come home to the limits of the historical. I am Everyman, unlimited and universal. But I am also only Sam Keen. Becker continues the tradition of thinkers like Kierkegaard, Wilhelm Reich, and Otto Rank that underlines the experience of limits and historicity. In this tradition the confrontation with death is the key to authentic life because death is the final and ineradicable limit. No matter how long the sentence wanders it must end with a period.

I have always felt there was something dishonest in the way mystics of an Eastern tinge dealt with death. They considered it only in terms of the death of the ego. Every time I face the necessity for a radical change in my life the specter of death appears. The fear that change means death lurks under the surface of consciousness and guards the fortress of conservatism. But when I pass through the death layer and the fear of change and surrender to the new thing that is trying to emerge in me, the fear of death retreats. The ego must die a thousand times before the self is born and each little death is a rite of passage into a larger life. I can agree with the ego-demolishers who see ego-death as a ritual promotion, a prelude to resurrection. *But that does not solve the problem of death.* There is the death that writes *finis,* that takes from us all we love, that strikes before or after we are prepared for it, that makes us fear Everyman's life story must be written as a tragedy. Ego-death is easy to celebrate after it has happened. The death that ends in cremation or burial is harder to affirm. Actual death may be a graduation to a higher level of being. But the fact is we do not know. And we fear it is the end and not the beginning. Any philosophy that does not deal with the fear of eradication seems inadequate. The cosmos may circle forever, renewing itself by feeding on its own tail, but there is something linear and fatally abrupt about human personality.

Becker's *Denial of Death* shows the shape of the character defenses we create in order to evade the terrifying knowledge of the inevitability of death. His work might be considered morbid if it weren't for the paradox: the more we face the fear of death the more we are freed to abandon ourselves to life.

I have thought much about death and been in its presence more than once. But nothing in theory or practice softened the impact of meeting and talking with Becker during his final battle with cancer. When it comes down to the fact, "death" is only a word for DEATH, and that phenomenon, like the face of God, is surrounded by an impenetrable mystery. I felt awed and honored to be invited into the intimacy of Earnest's dying. I spent only a day with him. We were friends so soon and for so short a time. Yet I will carry for a lifetime the images of that day: the courage, the clarity chosen at the cost of enduring pain, the triumph of trust in a time of desperately low energy. It is a privilege to have witnessed a heroic death.

Sometimes after the midpoint in life the quest for wisdom becomes attractive. As don Juan said, we need to be able to sum up our lives at any moment. Roberto Assagioli interests me because he has created a synthesis of techniques and points of view that supposedly leads to wisdom: psychosynthesis promises harmony. And that is a deal no one could resist. Or is it? As a philosopher I have, in theory, been searching for wisdom. But I sometimes suspect I don't want to find it. I seem to prefer passion, folly, and interesting mistakes to calm, harmony, and wisdom. My perverse relation to wisdom began early. My philosophical bent and my Presbyterian parents send me out on a premature quest. After I graduated from Jesus and the saints into existentialism and psychoanalysis, I began to suspect that a keen mind and a lot of knowledge had led me into caution and compulsion rather than toward freedom. Many thinking people in our culture suffer from the same irrational use of reason. A generation of careful and per-petual students has practiced moderation when it should have been immersed in excess. And many of us now approach the second half of life both needing wisdom and being reluctant to yield the moderate forms of excess we have won through "identity crises" and other much mini-madnesses. All of this is in the way of admitting that I approach Assagioli with one hopeful and one jaundiced eye.

I am happy enough to consider that there may be a reconciliation between warring opposites—reason and emotion, duty and desire, mind and body. I am tired of warfare. But reconciliation between the contradictions—psychosynthesis—makes sense only when the contradictions have been experienced. Hatred, cruelty, confusion, despair and madness must be admitted into consciousness before they can be integrated. I have to reverence my anger and my fear before they become civilized. In these years of transition I have not been nice. Repressed emotions or classes don't emerge politely. While I can look longingly at the promise of synthesis and harmony, my most creative discipline of the last years has been allowing disintegration. In the hero's journey there is a time of chaos when feelings burst free and contradictory passions run rampant.

But energy does need to be conserved, and every person and culture needs a time of synthesis. And perhaps it's coming together again. As a culture we have picked everything apart. Our preferred modes of knowledge have specialized in analysis and dissection, and we have neglected the unifying ways of feeling and intuition. Our knowledge has given us power, but the power has corrupted us. So now we need to begin moving toward a modern synthesis which will reunite machines and soil, analysis and intuition, inquiry and compassion, the hard head and the soft heart. I do not expect the synthesis to create a utopia or a final solution. Vital life will always involve a swing between chaos and order, adventure and security, and hence there will always be an oscillation between the disintegrative and the integrative tendencies of the human self. Western man has, like the prodigal son, been exiled in a far country, and it is now time to begin the journey home. It is time for scientists and mystics to join hands and for mechanics and visionaries to conspire together. I think this is what is beginning to happen.

Prophets and visionaries, whether true or false, arouse the instinct of hope and leave us wondering about the shape of the future. If tomorrow comes will it be like today, full of ambiguities and tragic dilemmas? Or may we expect a time of fulfillment, a homecoming in time? After this time of crisis what can we hope for?

My best hope for myself and America is that our disillusionment will deepen into maturity. Vietnam, Watergate, and our embattled ecology should have dispelled us of our illusions of innocence and righteous intentions. We have lost a war and watched the virtues of competition and efficiency turn into vices. The midlife crisis is upon us. We can no longer afford to squander our energies in adventures in foreign jungles or in reaching for the moon. We must now learn to shepherd our resources. The next generation faces the almost unthinkable task of:

limiting profit
voluntarily renouncing the politics of power
curtailing the cancerous rate of national growth (How gross the national product!)
changing from an economy of consuming to an economy of conservation
planning communities without yeilding to the Grand Inquisitor
reclaiming the body from over-civilization.

It is time, again, to study the ancient vision of the tragic sense of life, to search for a way to live joyfully within the limits of our mortality. We have lived as if we could consume endlessly, grow forever, and make unbroken progress. Suddenly we are up against the essential limitedness of life. There isn't time or energy for everything. Nor wealth enough on the planet for everyone to live endlessly like Americans. Maturity is the joyful acceptance of limits. It happens only after we have lost the illusion of inexhaustability.

I think there will be no alabaster cities undimmed by human tears. (I'm not certain I would want to live in one anyway.) Visions of Utopia are dangerous because they so easily destroy our ability to be satisfied by the limited reality of the everyday. The struggle for bread, for justice, and for a modicum of beauty will continue so long as there is history. No matter how hard our machines labor, the creation of a loving community will always exercise the human heart and hands to the fullest. Steel and computers wisely managed may produce a sufficiency for survival; they cannot create eros. So the best we can hope for is that every succeeding generation will keep alive the high and fragile vocation of struggling to create a more humane world.

Norman O. Brown's Body

A CONVERSATION WITH
NORMAN O. BROWN

Reprinted from PSYCHOLOGY TODAY Magazine, August, 1970.
Copyright © Ziff-Davis Publishing Company.

Brown, Prof. Norman O(liver), b. El Oro, Mex. Sept. 25, 1913. CLASSICAL PHILOLOGY, HISTORY, B.A. Oxford, 1936, Ph.D. U. Wis., 1942. Prof. langs., Nebr. Wesleyan Univ., 1942–43; from asst. prof. to Prof. of Classics, Wesleyan Univ. 1946–52; Prof. Classics & Comp. Lit., U. Rochester, 1962–68; now Prof. Humanities, Cowell Coll., U. Cal., Santa Cruz. U.S.A. 1943–45. Am. Philol. Assn., Class. Assn. New Eng. Mythology. Author: *Hermes the Thief, Life Against Death, Love's Body.* Address: Cowell College, U. Cal., Santa Cruz, 95060.

Norman O. Brown is variously considered the architect of a new view of man, a modern-day shaman, and a Pied Piper leading the youth of America astray. His more ardent admirers, of whom I am one, judge him one of the seminal thinkers who profoundly challenge the dominant assumptions of the age. Although he is a classicist by training who came late to the study of Freud and later to mysticism, he has already created a revolution in psychological theory. From his wooded retreat in the hills overlooking the Pacific at Santa Cruz he gently proclaims the coming apocalypse: "Permanent revolution, then, and no permanent (reified-visible) structures issuing from contract, commitment, promise, will or willpower, which are from the ego. Not voluntarism, but spontaneity, or grace; not the ego but the id."

27

Unsurprisingly, orthodox psychologists and educators have been able to restrain their enthusiasm for Brown. But the young, who hear the message of the end of the world as a hymn of hope for less repression, have made Brown a hero of the new order as they have Herbert Marcuse.

Brown begins his *Life Against Death* with the riddle that haunts all romantics: Why does man who is born into a garden of innocent delight create a culture in which he is alienated from himself, his fellows, and nature? Why civilization and its discontents instead of paradise? In the tradition of Nietzsche and Freud, Brown considers man a diseased animal. Culture emerges when erotic energy is sublimated and turned to the production of objects, character structures, and political organizations that yield little pleasure. Man alone of all the animals represses his true desires, lives in continual conflict and guilt, and constructs for himself a corporate neurosis that he calls civilization.

To solve the riddle of the perennial unhappy consciousness of man, Brown turns to Freud's notion of the conflict between Eros and Thanatos, the life instinct and death instinct. Neurosis arises from the incapacity to die, from a distortion of the death instinct; the distortion may be seen equally in the development of infants and in cultural institutions. The child perceives separation from the mother as abandonment and death and therefore refuses to admit the possibility. But in denying separation he also rejects his own potential individuality. Individualization, mortality, and the life of the body are inseparable. Thus the inability to affirm death carries with it the inability to enter into life.

Once the project of avoiding death is formed, the major amount of human energy is invested in the creation of reified-visible personality and political structures that foster the illusion that we are immune to change and death. Culture is a series of monuments inscribed with the motto "Death has no dominion." But death, the old black-clad Viet Cong warrior, will not be driven from his humus. The more he is denied and repressed, the more he absorbs our life-energies. And in the end Eros is destroyed and we become rigid and compulsive captives of the personalities, defense mechanisms and political institutions we have constructed to combat our enemy.

Brown's deviation from Freud begins to emerge when he sees a way beyond repression and built. Freud saw the warfare between Eros and Thanatos as perennial and could therefore suggest only a sad expedient—an alliance of ego and reality principle against the instinctual demands of the id. Brown, by contrast, suggests that we ally ego and id against the reality principle. He would create a new Dionysian man—erotic, playful, poetic and, in the awkward language of Freud, polymorphously perverse. This new man would enjoy the total body eroticism that is judged perverse under the restricted standards of adult genital sexuality but is natural in childhood. He would be strong enough to resurrect the body from the deadness that culture has imposed upon it. Without repression or guilt he could face death as the natural conclusion of a ripe mortal life. It is with this audacious proposal that Brown ends *Life Against Death.*

After he completed *Life Against Death,* something happened to Brown. The echo of the event is in his Phi Beta Kappa oration "Apocalypse—the Place of Mystery in the Life of the Mind" (published in *Harper's* Magazine, May 1961) in which he exalts enthusiasm and divine madness. The full measure of his conversion to the Dionysian way is obvious when one opens *Love's Body.* The old style is no more. Gone are the rational arguments supporting the end of argumentation, the prose defending poetry, the reasoned appeals for ecstasy. In their place are aphorism, poetry, and free association. Playfully and with abundant exaggeration Brown paints a portrait of the divinely inspired schizophrenic who transforms the world by poetic imagination and by his refusal to accept the boundaries that define the normal (or average) sense of reality.

It won't do to dismiss Brown as an unbalanced visionary. He

says worse of himself. He would be the first to admit the foolishness of his project. Indeed, he warns us at the beginning of *Life Against Death* that his effort to renew thought on the nature and destiny of man is unlikely to be "right" and is certain to insult common sense. But the question remains whether anything short of the madness Brown celebrates can save us from the certain destruction toward which the rational insanity of our technological culture is leading us. Perhaps a country that annually spends killions* of dollars to support the kingdom of death needs to hear paeans to Dionysus. The right kind of foolishness might save us from oblivion.

Warren Bennis:† I would like to begin by exploring some of the connections between your imagination and your experience. How did it happen that a classical scholar became the chief architect of a new Dionysian view of man and one of the most widely discussed psychological theorists of our time? From what crucible of experience did your ideas emerge?

Norman Brown: I had always been interested in mythology and had in *Hermes the Thief* given a rather successful sociological interpretation greatly influenced by Marx. And I was on the point of settling down to a lifetime of sociological interpretation of mythology. Then suddenly I encountered both blockage in classical scholarship and catastrophe in the outside world of politics. I found I couldn't interpret myth adequately with sociological categories. Thus in the early fifties I discovered Freud with shock and intensity. You see I came late to the dilemma of my generation. Others such as Leslie Fiedler had been naturally breathing the air of both Marx and Freud since the late thirties. My intense involvement with Freud in *Life Against Death* reflects the surprise of a latecomer to what many people have known for a long time. And I suspect the same is true of that second

---

*Killion—a monetary unit to measure "defense" spending.
†As mentioned in the Introduction, the conversation was done jointly by Warren Bennis and Sam Keen. It appears here under Bennis' name for the sake of clarity.

shift in my thinking, let's say loosely from psychoanalysis to a more mystical direction, which took place from *Life Against Death* to *Love's Body*. There again I was discovering what some of my contemporaries such as John Cage had discovered twenty years earlier. I see myself as being a late learner like Augustine when in *The Confessions* he says, "Late I learnt to love thee, Beauty, as ancient as thou art new; late I learnt to love thee."

Bennis: There often seems to occur in the creative man an upheaval, something akin to Erik Erikson's identity crisis, but rather than afflicting the adolescent it comes much later in life. It is what I call a destination crisis. Augustine, Freud, Shaw, and Gandhi all experienced great reversals at about the age of forty. What happened when you were forty? You mentioned earlier some political upheavals. Was this the Henry Wallace campaign?

Brown: Yes. My emotional and ideological involvement in the hopes and dreams of the Left continued through the year 1948 and the campaign of Henry Wallace. Until that time I held the enlightenment view that man has a limitless capacity to perfect himself by manipulating his environment. From my disillusionment with that election I drew the conclusion that there was something seriously wrong with the premises and understanding of human nature and society with which I had been operating up to that time.

I began then a long process, which is culminated in *Love's Body*, of facing up to the unchanging aspects of human nature and the darkness that is an abiding part of the human condition. One of the good metaphors in *Love's Body* is that it is always daybreak, not noon as some social scientists and enlightenment thinkers claim. This meant for me a deep withdrawal—from any kind of political participation. In order to do the kind of thinking that seemed to me necessary, I had to be a nonparticipant. In this long, agonizing crisis, which continues, I have been engaged in asking myself what was wrong with the thoughts I had when I was a young man. You see, I am a late learner whose theme song is a palinode or recantation saying, "I was wrong."

Bennis: Dr. Brown, I would like to know more of your early life and family background. Your book is fugitive here—indeed, almost mute. "Norman O. Brown was born in 1913 in Mexico, where his father was a mining engineer. He was educated at Oxford, University of Chicago and the University of Wisconsin where he took his doctorate in 1942 . . ."

Brown: O.K., skip the rest. That I owe to goofy public-relations people who tried to make me mysterious. But it does, as accidents often do, reflect a certain liking for anonymity. Let me try to overcome it. I think the Biblical archetype of exodus and exile has been fundamental to my life. By an unlikely conjunction of accidents I was born in Mexico. My father, a poor younger son, set off to make his fortune as a mining engineer in Mexico. On the boat he met my mother who was one-half German, one-quarter Spanish and one-quarter Peruvian Indian. She had been raised in Germany and was going to visit relatives in Havana. Your speculations about the psychodynamics of the marriage are as good as mine. I picture it as some strange madness underneath the Caribbean moon. At any rate, the family soon returned to England so my sister and I could be educated. After that I suppose the most decisive gesture in my life was my flight from England to the United States in 1936. I left my motherland and my mother and father and did not see them again for more than twenty-five years. There was no quarrel or rupture but there was a deep and permanent separation.

This exile seems to me a true metaphor of the way I find myself in life. I fell in love with my new-found-land—America. I think that in England I would have died for lack of cultural and intellectual space. And I do believe in the future of America far more than I believe in the future of Europe. America means to me the possibility of open space, of clearing away the rubbish of the past. And yet I guess I'm contradicting myself about being an exile. I'm saying both that I'm in love with this country and that I feel everywhere an exile. America then and now symbolizes to me a climate, spiritual and cultural, in which it is possible to think about what it would mean to bring an end to that nightmare which is history.

Bennis: Your longing for a post-historical community is well-expressed in *Life Against Death* where you renounce the reality principle for the pleasure principle. In describing the new man who would no longer be governed by repression you say that he would have a Dionysian consciousness and would delight in the full life of the body. Unlike the Apollonian man he would neither negate nor observe limits. Could we say that in *Love's Body* you have given a concrete constitution, in poetic form, for a nonrepressed, Edenic community? Some students have seen *Love's Body* as a manual for revolution, a guidebook for bringing in the New Jerusalem.

Brown: If I accepted responsibility for the interpretations that might be put on my work I would have been paralyzed. I did feel when writing *Love's Body* some kind of obligation to undo what I had done in *Life Against Death*. I wanted to release any followers I had acquired or at least to confuse them. Insofar as *Life Against Death* happened to end up by making me a leader, I did want to get lost. I don't want to be a leader. Let me suggest an analogy. Shelley's poem "The Cloud" is about the metamorphosis of a cloud. "I bring fresh showers for the thirsting flowers," etc., but it is the last two lines that I identify with: "I silently laugh at my own cenotaph and arise and unbuild it again." I laugh at my own cenotaph. The previous book is a cenotaph. It is my grave, for I am no longer there. The grave is empty and, like the ghost in Hamlet, I like to travel underground and appear someplace else. Thus I felt under some existential stress to write *Love's Body* in order to torpedo *Life Against Death,* to destroy it as a position. And therefore in one sense to disclose that I am self-contradictory, that is to say an unstable person whom you should not trust. I wanted to release students from a position that might bind them.

Bennis: I don't understand how *Love's Body* torpedoes the position you take in *Life Against Death*. I see little contradiction between the two books. It would seem to me, to the contrary, that sometime after *Life Against Death* you became converted by your own message and adopted the poetic, aphoristic style that is the appropriate means of expression for a Dionysian thinker.

Brown: One goes so far and so one has to go further. *Love's Body* is an explanation of the meaning of "the resurrection of the body" which appears as an abstract slogan in *Life Against Death*. But the meaning of love's body turned out to be different from that anticipated by the author of *Life Against Death*—much more poetical, much less political.

Bennis: I have wondered whether you stop short of the implications of your own vision of the Dionysian style of life. You propose doing away with the repressed, genitally organized personality that has characterized Western man and returning erotic consciousness to the whole body. You then reach what is to me a strange conclusion when you define poetry—wordplay—as the most appropriate expression of the polymorphously perverse, or Dionysian, way of life. Why not sensitize and eroticize the actual carnal body? Wouldn't the reeducation of touch, taste, smell, and hearing lead more quickly to an erotic view of reality than wordplay?

Brown: The point at which *Love's Body* ends is the identity of deed and word, word and flesh; recovering the original meaning of poetry which is actual making or doing, a bodily gesture. That is poetical, isn't it? In other words, the distinction presupposed in your question between poetry and the carnal body, between imagination and sensation, may be precisely what has to be overcome.

Bennis: Perhaps this is an unfair question, but I will ask it anyway, since it is a matter of constant speculation by your readers. To what degree are you able to live out the vision you articulate in *Love's Body?* Are you polymorphously perverse?

Brown: I have been told that students who meet me in the classroom often say, "Why doesn't he practice what he preaches?" In my own case I perceive a necessary gap between seeing and being. I would not be able to have said certain things if I had been under the obligation to unify the word and the deed. As it is I can let my words reach out and net impossible things—things that are impossible for me to do. And this is a way of paying the price for saying or seeing things.

You will remember that I discovered these things as a late learner. Polymorphous perversity in the literal, physical sense is not the real issue. I don't like the suggestion that polymorphous perversity of the imagination is somehow second-best to literal polymorphous perversity. You know there is one quotation from William Blake that I repeated at least three times in *Love's Body* and that says, "The Eternal Body of Man *is* the imagination. . . ." The primary issue, or if Blake is right, the whole issue, is in the imagination. Polymorphous perversity turns out to be a poetical rather than a literal thing. It is a form of mental playfulness as in *Finnegans Wake,* something I do with my mind, a changed way of seeing that I would like to carry into everything I see.

Bennis: Would you say that the widespread use of LSD and other hallucinogenic drugs has given the present generation an unprecedent acquaintance with the Dionysian style of life? Some have claimed that LSD creates instant polymorphous perversity.

Brown: I don't accept the standard use of the word "hallucinogenic." I don't like hallucinogenic things such as the mass media with their advertising and political campaigns, with their managed and manufactured news. I don't use drugs. However, it is obvious that we need a breakthrough to a visionary reality, poetic vision. Surely the Second Coming is at hand, when your young men shall see visions.

Bennis: While we are on personal questions, I would like to ask about your own experience in psychoanalysis. I'm curious. Have you ever been analyzed?

Brown: Since I am trying to overcome my reticence and strain in the direction of autobiographical disclosure, I think I should say that I have never been in analysis. So *Life Against Death* is an attack on my father Freud, who claimed that none but he could do it without being analyzed. With a kind of Protestant or Promethean arrogance I did it myself. More recently, as life and age catch up with me, I realize that one pays a price for doing it this way. Working my way by myself through psychoanalysis has not given me anything that could be called peace of mind. In fact—here's another disclosure for your interpretation—it gave me insomnia. Until I wrote *Life Against Death* I was a perfect sleeper. But when I learned to interpret my dreams the power to dream or to sleep was taken from me. Freud said he came to disturb the sleep of the world. In my case he succeeded.

Bennis: Both you and Freud came at the unconscious—at the terror that is present when repression is lifted—by your intellectual powers. You more or less backed into it by interpreting myths and dreams.

Brown: Well, one is seduced into it, and if one had known in advance what one was getting into, I suppose one wouldn't have done it. I have been very impressed, when I look back on my own experience, by how *Life Against Death* was started in a spirit of almost absurd play of ideas, as if one could explore these ideas and not get hurt by pure play. But I've been impressed to the extent that one gets sentenced by one's own sentences. One explores certain things in play and then in a strange way they become commitments with which one has to live. I have gained a deep respect for the demonic power of the word. Words are not idle. They have consequences.

Bennis: Let's change directions for a moment. A great number of the more revolutionary students find themselves caught between an impulse toward political activism, which is nurtured by Marcuse, and a metapolitical life-style that seems to be recommended by *Love's Body*. In your exchange in *Commentary* in 1967, Marcuse accuses you of mystification and of refusal to deal with concrete political strategies that would lead to a less repressive society. Your reply was that "the next generation needs to be told that the real fight is not the political fight, but to put an end to politics. From politics to metapolitics. From politics to poetry." Would you comment on the issues that separate you from Marcuse? Or to put the question in another way, in what way is poetry revolutionary?

Brown: I tried to answer this question in my Atherton lecture at Harvard "From Politics to Metapolitics" (published in *Caterpillar* No. 1) in which I explored the idea of a visionary, poetic, and metapolitical revolution. Politics is fratricide or suicide. That is the first chapter in *Love's Body;* that is the situation we now have, the situation from which we are trying to escape. The obstacles preventing unification of the body politic are political divisions and boundaries. But at a deeper level it is the reality principle, the boundary between Self and Other, the logic which divides, which most people think is reason itself, or rationality. Poetry and dialectical thought overthrow the reality principle, unite the opposites and transform this world in a deeper sense.

I am not specially pleased with this lecture. My generation has been haunted by the following riddle: When is a revolution not a revolution? Serious thought on the relation between poetry and revolution would take us deep into the nature of the Russian Revolution and the Cultural Revolution of Mao.

Bennis: Would you put an end to science as well as politics? Or can science also become poetic?

Brown: I am not a scientist, but I have a deep suspicion that the nature of science has been misunderstood by scientists. I draw comfort from T. S. Kuhn's *The Structure of Scientific Revolutions.* The real creative scientists, as opposed to the codifiers and appliers who come in the wake of the breakthroughs and write them up in textbooks, are both revolutionary and poetic. Science is not opposed to poetry.

Bennis: Every great breakthrough in science, every scientific revolution, has also been a poetic revolution because it has created a new paradigm of thought.

Brown: Yes, the breakthrough depends upon the perception of some new organizing metaphor.

Bennis: And the debureaucratization of the imagination. So it's a replacement of the metaphor and a new way of opening up restructuring. I think Freud is perhaps the best example of this.

Brown: Perhaps you're being a little evasive with that word "debureaucratization" because what Freud and other creative scientists do is quite violent and I'm not sure you can have a peaceful transition of debureaucratization. I think there is some kind of inevitable upheaval. So both science and poetry ought to be in some condition of permanent revolution.

Bennis: Right, but where is poetry today? How do you get poetry in the disciplines?

Brown: I'm much encouraged by my efforts in this last stretch of my life since I wrote *Love's Body*. I'm trying to make Clio a muse again, to make history poetic again. I find there are great possibilities even in the university to make the wilderness of the social sciences bloom, to make poetry there. The most meaningful poetry can be made in those areas of thought at the university that are so aridly prosaic. And to have a Sunday-afternoon performance by a visiting poet is no solution to the wickedness of the week.

Bennis: That reminds me of those lectures on Man you always see on stencil posted in the student union. Man is banished from the classroom and relegated to Sunday evenings.

Brown: I think there is a deep connection between poetry and freedom. It was the psychoanalytic principle of free association that alerted me to the relation between wordplay and freedom. I think a poetic classroom is one where poetry is created by freedom and free associations. I notice that my own lectures are tending to become a kind of collage in which the students or the audience participate.

Bennis: So the classroom might become almost like a group collage of ideas.

Brown: Yes. And if this means loss of the sense of private property of ideas so much the better.

Bennis: True science should be nonpossessive anyway.

Brown: I think so. If you believe in the ubiquity of genius, as you have to if you follow either Freud or Blake, then there are unharvested treasures in any collection of people.

Bennis: What about your future? Where do you go from here? What will the post-apocalyptic, post-*Love's Body* Norman Brown look like?

Brown: I wrote a preface to *Love's Body* which in a very short space says three times "This is the end." I'm not sure what that means. I think it means no more metaphysical overview flights in my career. In some sense I have come down to earth and the work I want to do from now on is concrete work with particulars, which is also for me poetry. Poetry I think is made with particulars, not with abstractions. I'm trying to get away from abstractions in my work and to poetize particular areas. I rather like a thing I have done called "Daphne, or Metamorphosis," published in *Myths, Dreams, and Religion* edited by Joseph Campbell. My work also returns to politics. I would like to do a poetics of politics, a poetic approach to the structure of civilization. However, my experience is that the unexpected keeps breaking through. Thank God! Real discoveries are always surprises. I may yet be surprised—again.

Civilization and Eros

A CONVERSATION WITH HERBERT MARCUSE

Reprinted from PSYCHOLOGY TODAY Magazine, February, 1971.

"Mar-coo-za, Mar-coo-za"

The hall is jammed with students. More gather outside around loudspeakers. One group bangs on the doors chanting, "Mar-coo-za, Mar-coo-za, Mar-coo-za." A tall man hunches over the podium waiting for the clamor to subside. He seems no fiery prophet and certainly no wild revolutionary; his body is aging and his eyes are tired. But then his rich voice reaches out and his charisma radiates. He tells of freedom and oppression, labor and love, of how art, sexuality and reason itself are enslaved by the work culture. He imagines an erotic world of play and joy, where man, nature, and music will be spontaneous and free. He damns the "progressive moronization of humanity," and applause thunders. It is a familiar scene in a dozen countries, where, to his surprise and delight, the 72-year-old prophet from Berlin finds himself honored by questing and militant youth.

Herbert Marcuse's life has been full. Privileged son of an affluent Jewish family, he studied literature during his youth. After activist Army days he became disillusioned with the German revolution and turned to studies in philosophy. He received a Ph.D. from the University of Freiburg in 1922 and, like Sartre, became Martin Heidegger's assistant. Later, tantalized by the unorthodox ideas of young Wilhelm Reich, he joined the Institute for Social Research in Geneva at the invitation of T. W. Adorno and Max Horkheimer when Nazism forced him to leave

43

Germany in 1933. After a year he immigrated to the United States, taught at Columbia, and became a citizen in 1940. During World War II he worked for the Office of Strategic Services and later in the State Department. In 1951 he resumed his academic career at Columbia, Harvard, and Brandeis, then, in 1965, moved to the University of California at San Diego.

Now he lives with his wife Inge in a tract house in La Jolla on the edge of the U.C.S.D. campus where he instructs graduate students in philosophy. Serene in old age, he puffs cigars, basks in the La Jolla sunshine and is intrigued by the inpouring of threat and abuse.

The *New York Times Magazine* has given him double billing as "the angel of the apocalypse" and "the most important philosopher alive." His writings with their twin themes of reason and eros begin to tell us why. In *Reason and Revolution* (1941) he explains Hegel's position to have been that a decisive turn in history came when, with the French Revolution, modern man first discovered reason's potential for challenging existing society. In *Eros and Civilization* (1955) he rejects Freud's thesis that while the infant's whole body is erotic, biological development and socialization must *necessarily* channel eroticism toward genital sexuality, thus releasing the rest of the body for the impersonal work of civilization. Marcuse claims that while this has been historically true it need not continue to be so, since a careful application of technology could now free man from scarcity and stuporous work. Like Marx he is convinced that once freed, man could awaken to new sensibilities. He could become playful and gentle, erotic in all his dimensions, no longer enamored of conquest, adventure, and power. However, in *Soviet Marxism* (1958) he describes Stalinist Soviet reality as a brutal bureaucratization of Marx's humanistic vision.

In *One-Dimensional Man* (1964), his most popular work, he abjures today's technological states, arguing that all-encompassing affluence dulls the sensitivities and that the vaunted new sexuality is at best a sapping diversion and at worst an ally of profit and manipulation. He despairs at the extent to which all aspects of existence are co-opted by the repressive bureaucratic ethic. Even free time, art, and play are harnessed to re-create energy needed for the enervating work of servicing the technoculture. How can this situation be changed? In an essay that troubles traditional liberals, "Repressive Tolerance" (1965), he gives some hints by modifying John Stuart Mill's contention that changes in social structure and values must occur only after discussion and testing in the marketplace of ideas. Marcuse reasons that this makes sense only if all participants in the discussion are rational, informed, and free from indoctrination. That condition does not exist, for everywhere radical dissent is co-opted or repressed. To redress the situation, those who preach racism, hatred, and intolerance should be restrained in turn. Finally, in *An Essay on Liberation* (1969), by far his most hopeful statement, he asserts that some youthful and alienated members of society —militant students and black people—are nurturing seeds of a new sensibility from which nonrepressive Utopia might eventually blossom.

Such ideas have stirred a prodigious uproar. He has been portrayed in *National Review* as an "apostle of chaos" and condemned by Arthur Schlesinger for extolling primitive emotion over restraint and reason. The American Legion demands that he be fired. Letters signed "K.K.K." have threatened his life. *Pravda* has damned him as a "false prophet" and "a werewolf." Sidney Hook sneers that "Marcuse would ruthlessly suppress all who disagree with him about how to make man and society freer"; Erich Fromm writes, "Marcuse seems to imply that because perversions—like sadism or coprophilia—cannot result in procreation, they are more 'free' than genital sexuality"; while *Fortune* deplores his "lush, cosmic, romanticism" which "reverberates ominously through the corridors of our time."

It figures. Critics like Hook and Fromm, despite their Marxism and humanism, do not really challenge the most fundamental premises of existing morality. Marcuse does. Like Picasso's later drawings, Marcuse's utopian thought conveys with bold strokes a vision of the erotic possibilities of human life. His concept of man as a playful animal longing to unfold his sensuous nature is not apt to delight *Pravda,* the K.K.K. or totalitarian moralists of any stripe. Then too, youths have found in Marcuse an eloquent voice for their instinctive disdain of the performance culture. So the troubled elders naturally view Marcuse, like Socrates, as a corrupter of the young. And indeed his writings can spur action. By confirming the feelings of those already disillusioned with industrial society's failure to nurture freedom, he furnishes the ideological genesis for developing alternative life-styles. But finally, much resistance to Marcuse is based not so much on his writings as upon his radical political stances. He champions student militants against the Establishment. He decries "increasing repression" under the Nixon Administration. He refuses to turn his back on his former pupil Angela Davis. His consistent espousal of radical action is an offense to liberals who have opted for sensible gradualism and modification rather than eradication of the political culture. He even puts down the triple consciousness of Charles Reich.

We come still closer to the man if we fall into the rhythm of his days. Eavesdrop as he admonishes a friend about his motorcycle because "it is a fascist invention which equates speed and power with virility and besides it makes a dreadful noise and pollutes terribly." Spot him in a peace march, protesting unacclaimed. Listen to the whirring air conditioner in his ugly cement-and-steel office join the roar of jets in drowning out his voice as he says, "We must get rid of our present cities." Watch the give and take as he engages his rich and disciplined mind with the probing ones of his students, leading them into new dimensions of awareness. Discover him strolling beneath the cliffs on Torrey Pines Beach hand in hand with his wife. Observe his courtly joking with the secretaries who provide the final barrier against the always curious and often hostile public. He overflows with a joyous lustiness, with eros if you will.

Eros is the key to this thought. His work is grounded in Freud's concepts of Eros and Thanatos, the instinct for life and the seduction of easeful death. But Freud was obsessed with civilization's repression of the life instinct; Marcuse dreams of a miracle of reason and imagination whereby man could escape his bondage as a work animal and search out the road to Utopia. Hegel fathered his commitment to reason—the *logos*. It is reason that arbitrates Eros and Thanatos. Through reason the death instinct can be sublimated to the service of life. Through reason men can learn to throw off the shackles of repression. And then through reason liberated man can use science and art to create a society in which eroticism can pervade his whole being and flood his relationships with nature and with his fellows. But this eroticism is not the rampantly self-seeking sexuality described by Freud, nor is it the metaphorical union of all fancied by Norman Brown. It is instead a "creative human existence" disciplined by reason, enriched with passion, suffused with joy. Repressive and alienating socieites transcended, man could fully develop his sensibilities and flower in all his dimensions. His body could be transformed into an instrument of pleasure; his mind could expand to higher levels of consciousness: psyche and *logos* could bloom.

In some ways Marcuse's visions of revolution and Utopia differ little from fundamentalist dreams of redemption and heaven. He lives within a curious boundary. He is a philosopher in the European romantic tradition and his thought is largely unaffected by the work of natural and behavioral scientists, from Charles Darwin to Loren Eiseley, who have begun to explore the sometimes brutal evolutionary drive-mechanisms by which life seeks ever more complexity, ever new frontiers of consciousness. Nor does his Utopia reflect the growing evidence that love and aggression are not really in opposition, but are fundamentally entwined in society, in the psyche, and even in the body's chemistry. Untouched by these new visions of the dynamic of life, Marcuse is restricted to Marx's "end of history" and Freud's "infantile sexuality." He almost seems to want a world in which man will not respond joyously to challenge, risk and danger. Can he really picture a natural order in which "animals do not eat each other"? If so, isn't he indeed dreaming of a final haven and the end of evolution's embattled quest? Is his eroticism then a closed circle, trapped in immanence, going nowhere? Or, on the other hand, how can we be sure that once they are liberated, man's erotic instincts will not run wild?

The deeper you go in questions with him, the more he enlivens the imagination. His vision may be limited, but it is luminous and steady. It is a vision of man at last using his vast capacities and accomplishments to maximize human joy. And "without vision," said an earlier prophet, "the people perish."

John Raser
Professor of Political Philosophy
Claremont Graduate School

Herbert Marcuse: I hope you don't intend to ask me about my theories or writings. It is useless for me to try to elaborate what I have written. If I could have said it more clearly I would have; I still try. Nor do I think it will be particularly interesting to talk about my private psyche. I have never been analyzed. I apparently didn't need it. Psychologically, I hope, I am not interesting at all. I am fairly normal.

Sam Keen: As a public phenomenon you seem to have sprung full-grown from the head of Zeus. Suddenly students in rebellion all over the world have claimed Herbert Marcuse as an ally and a major prophet of their hoped-for new age. What events nurtured your passionate commitment to a revolutionary analysis of the modern world?

Marcuse: Well obviously it didn't spring from the head of Zeus, although it might seem like it since my books have only recently become popular here and in Europe. As a young student I read Marx and what was then considered avant-garde literature.

Keen: Do you remember a time when you were not an intensely political and philosophical human being? What created your passion?

Marcuse: My passion came from my personal experience of the betrayal and defeat of the German revolution and the organization of the fascist counterrevolution which eventually brought Hitler to power. I was twenty when the German revolution broke out. I was in the last half-year of my army service and was stationed in Berlin. I got my first revolutionary experience as a member of a Soldiers' Council, but it was a brief experience because the revolution was quickly betrayed.

In 1919, I think, I left Berlin and went to Freiburg where I became absorbed in my studies of comparative literature, philosophy and economics. I was relatively dormant politically for the next fourteen years until I left Germany in 1933 and joined the Institute for Social Research in Geneva. During the year at the Institute my political passion was reawakened under the influence of my colleagues Max Horkheimer and T. W. Adorno. After my immigration to America in 1934, these men, along with Hegel, Marx, and Freud, continued to be the dominant influences upon my thought. Recently there were differences between Horkheimer and myself.

Keen: What were these differences?

Marcuse: We have different evaluations of the worldwide student movement and of the character of American politics. I see in the student movement a vital social and political force; my friends are reluctant to do so. They see America as a progressive and even liberal society compared to the Soviet Union. While I agree with their condemnation of the Soviet regime and agree that there are still progressive and liberal forces active in U.S. society, I see U.S. policies, domestic as well as foreign, as systematically repressive of human freedom.

John Raser: We know that the antithesis between repression and freedom is one cornerstone of your thought, and that you believe that a radical restructuring of society is necessary to end repression and to liberate the human psyche. But short of this utopian restructuring of society, do you see any role for psychotherapy in sowing the seeds of liberation? Or do you think that therapy as it is currently conceived and practiced is in effect conformist, privatistic, and antirevolutionary?

Marcuse: Obviously if psychiatry merely helps the patient adjust to a sick society so that he can function in it, it only moves him from one kind of sickness to another. Even Freud admitted this, but rejected the idea that psychoanalysts should make patients into revolutionaries or rebels against their society. Freud as a person may have been bourgeois and conservative. Yet his theory contains transcending radical elements. So you cannot say that Freudian theory and practice are either conformist or nonconformist. They are both, and I think—although Freud would reject this—that his decisive concepts are definitely revolutionary.

Keen: I think that Freud, like Melville, was haunted by dreams of both the easy freedom of the South Seas and the chaotic terror of the peasant revolution.

Raser: Perhaps traditional American psychiatry suffers from the same defect as Freud in that it almost totally ignores the political implications of its theory. Only you, Norman O. Brown, and perhaps Erik Erikson, have been willing to deal seriously with the political implications of Freud's analysis of the repressed and liberated psyche.

Marcuse: But a problem arises here. American society generates a lot of pathology among individuals. It creates a lot of psychic casualties. Therefore American psychiatrists have been overwhelmed with the need to treat patients who simply cannot function. If a person cannot digest, if he cannot eat, these functions have to be restored and politics and social consciousness have to be excluded unless they become essential for the therapy. Just as a physician need not ask about the moral or political opinions of a patient in order to cure him of pneumonia, so a psychiatrist usually need not treat the specific politics of a patient in order to cure him of some psychosomatic illness.

You just can't say generally whether psychiatry is politically reactionary or conformist.

Raser: You mean in theory. You can, I think, in practice.

Marcuse: In what sense?

Raser: In its fee structure, in its privatism, in its emphasis on the correction of pathology rather than the stimulation of growth, and in its habit of adjusting people to the existing world of work and social injustice. I think one telling indication of the apolitical stance of American therapists is evident in the fate of Wilhelm Reich. Reich insisted upon a marriage between Freud and Marx, the body and the body politic. But American Reichians have all but ignored Reich's political insights and claimed only his analysis of the physical dynamics of character structure.

Keen: That may be a rather pessimistic view. I think there are some revolutionary implications in the whole movement toward group therapy. Psychology is becoming more popular and vulgar in a positive sense. Don't you agree?

Marcuse: I must tell you that anything I say about group therapy is an impertinence because I have not studied it. I know about encounter and gestalt groups only from reports of the kinds of things that go on there. I read the catalogs of the Esalen Institute. To me this is sufficient to be horrified. This administration of happiness is nauseating to me. They teach people to touch each other and hold hands! If somebody cannot learn that by himself, by trial and error, he may just as well give up.

Raser: But in point of fact a lot of people in our society are afraid to reach out and touch others. They remain isolated, lonely, and insensitive.

Marcuse: Then they are not going to be helped by learning these things in a contrived and mechanical way. Such things have to come out of a person, as his or her own, without organization.

Raser: Let me offer a slightly different perspective about the significance of these sensitivity and encounter groups. It is a similar argument used by some apologists for LSD. If a person has grown up in a society where from infancy his fantasies and sensibilities have been stifled, he may not even know what forms of imagination and intimacy are possible. Some people have claimed that the hallucinogenics draw aside the curtain screening off a rich world of imagination. In a similar way people in these groups can learn how to reach out and touch others.

Marcuse: But you are always being touched today and slapped on the shoulder and all of that whether you want it or not.

Keen: But if a competitive society destroys tenderness and intimacy then perhaps we have to use contrived means to reawaken them.

Marcuse: I may be very wrong but I feel that a human being has to learn some things by himself. If someone has to study a textbook on sexual behavior in order to learn how to make love to his wife or girl, something is wrong with him.

Keen: The analysis of shame you make in *An Essay on Liberation* seems to bear on this subject. You say that a capitalistic society takes the Oedipal situation and compounds it by authoritarian political and economic structures, and thus psychological and political repression creates a personality that is deeply shamed and guilt-ridden. If shame and guilt cut us off from our sensibilities, doesn't it follow that a revolutionary form of therapy would have to de-shame the individual?

How do you suggest that we go about the process of de-shaming?

Marcuse: I think you have brought up the decisive point. I would say that shame is something positive and authentic. There are qualities and dimensions of the human being that are his own possessions —and I mean that in a nonexploitative and nonacquisitive way. They are his own and he shares them only with those whom he chooses. They do not belong to the community and they are not a public affair.

Keen: But you seem to be implying that only shame would protect privacy. Surely it is possible for an individual—a human being—to have privacy without shame.

Marcuse: I don't see how. If, for example, you are supposed to have a sexual relationship with someone before the eyes of the group, this is a regressive and repressive development. This is even true for something as minor as holding hands. If that must be rehearsed in a group the authentic erotic element is lost.

Raser: I would like to argue with you a bit on the basis of personal experience in such groups. The kind of competitive society in which we live makes it very difficult, for instance, for a man to accept his feeling of intimacy and warmth for another man.

Marcuse: Yes, that is true.

Raser: Almost all our male-to-male relationships are hostile and distant or involve a backslapping, shallow friendship game. As D. H. Lawrence said, men don't even know how to be friends without risking homosexual panic. Well, in these groups I have learned through contrived little exercises directed by clever people to own some of my warm, erotic feelings for other men.

Marcuse: You speak now only for other men? Would you say the same for a man-woman or woman-woman relationship?

Raser: Surely. My experience is that some of these new therapeutic techniques can aid in increasing the erotic component of *all* relationships and can help to create the new sensibilities about which you write so eloquently. Having allowed yourself to be open in a protected environment that says, "It is O.K. for you to experiment with new ways of seeing and being," then you have opened that window to the new sensibilities.

Marcuse: Yes, but only if you already have them within yourself.

Raser: I think people do, but society forces us to repress them. I am not talking about generating emotions, but about liberating those that have long been denied and twisted. I think I have learned much of this from your own writings.

Keen: In this sense the therapist is like the Zen master—a kind of trickster who says, "I give you permission to do something that you really don't need permission to do."

Marcuse: Yes, you are quite right. I said from the beginning that I was impertinent to talk about such matters. But if I give you my spontaneous reactions I must come back to what I said before. There is for me in all of this something too didactic. The teacher is saying, "Be real, natural. Feel more." You know I am very much in favor of learning. Some people say, probably correctly, that I am very authoritarian. But there are just some dimensions of human existence where the concept of organized teaching and learning seems to be inapplicable. Well, I really don't want to pass judgment. This is one of my prejudices. I consider it a prejudice. Maybe the groups are right and I am wrong. I don't know.

Raser: When we talk about psychic health as involving the release of repressed sensibilities that may be threatening to social norms then we raise the question as to what we mean by sanity. An emerging motif in therapy stresses the positive value of madness—of minipsychoses as breakthrough experiences that permit reintegration of the psyche on a higher level. For some, the criterion of successful therapy has become how crazy and autonomous—how independent of ordinary social controls—the patient becomes. R. D. Laing, for instance, sees adjustment to society as sick. You must surely consider this a radical approach to therapy.

Marcuse: Well, I met Laing, but we seem to be unable to find common ground. I am certainly opposed to any trend which glorifies nuts just because they are nuts. Certainly you will not help society by making people crazier than they are. What you get is only a society with one craziness against another craziness. There is a kind of craziness you need if you are going to work in a revolutionary way within a repressive society without being crushed by it. But this form of madness cannot be produced by psychiatry. It is a madness of the *logos* and is highly rational. It involves insight into the basic ills of society and analysis of the ways and means at your disposal for changing things. So I don't see why you have to make people crazy in order to make them rebels against their society. To the contrary, any person with his five senses intact and with a more or less developed consciousness should be able to become a rebel without any help at all from a psychiatrist.

Keen: In *An Essay on Liberation* you talk about the need to develop both a new sensibility and a new rationality. Wouldn't the new sensibility include a deeper appreciation of the unconscious, of the playful and irrational dimension of the mind? This might release a motive power—a joyousness, if you like—that may not be characteristic of the pure rationality and analysis that you see as the major faculties of the rebel.

Marcuse: Yes, but this development of the new consciousness and of the new sensibility is in itself a rational process which cannot be attained artificially or synthetically. Liberation, for instance, cannot be achieved through drugs. They may provide the individual occasion, the starting shock, but the effect can only be sustained by translating the chemical reaction into political commitment. The real emancipation of man can take place only in a different society after a fundamental change in values and in political and economic structures. Now here is a paradox, for I have always insisted that this new rationality and sensibility must emerge *prior* to the change. They are necessary to bring about the change. We cannot possibly expect human beings who have been distorted and mutilated by being born into and living in this society to set up new institutions and relationships that are really liberating and emancipating. In other words—and perhaps this softens the paradox—at least some human beings with new values and new aspirations must exist and do their work *prior* to the massive change that will make general liberation possible.

Raser: It sounds suspiciously like the old problem of the chicken and the egg. Where will such virgin consciousness come from in a tainted society?

Marcuse: What do you mean, where will they come from? They are already here. I see this new type emerging in the young, especially among the students. The militant kids have made this transvaluation of values. They do not accept the established values of the society. They are, so far as I know them, totally nonviolent and nonaggressive in their instincts. They feel they know that with the resources available we could create a decent society almost from one day to the next, were it not for the overwhelming power of the Establishment.

Raser: You say you don't think drugs are responsible for this new sensibility on the part of the young. What might be?

Marcuse: We know fairly well what has articulated it in this country. This new attitude started in the early sixties when many of these kids went down to the South and saw for the first time how American democracy and equality were really functioning. It was a traumatic shock to them. Then came the war in Southeast Asia as the second traumatic shock. Now repression at home and abroad has been fortified by the Nixon Administration. So I don't think you have to ask for any artificial or mysterious explanations of the new militancy. It is what you should expect from kids who are not integrated into this society, who are not yet willing to sell out. It is frequently said that the militant students are a spoiled, privileged, middle-class elite. That is only true to a very limited extent. And even to the extent that it is true it is precisely this privileged position which gives them enough distance and dissociation from the society to be anguished rather than absorbed by it.

Keen: How important do you think the presence of the nuclear specter has been in creating disillusionment with the old values and stirring up search for the new?

Raser: A young girl I know recently said, "The bomb has fallen and we are the mutations."

Marcuse: Excellent. She is quite right. However, I think the threat of nuclear war is by no means the worst thing we are facing. It is quite possible that the superpowers will come to an agreement not to use nuclear weapons in their own interests. The real catastrophe is the prospect of total moronization, dehumanization, and manipulation of man.

Keen: In a strange way the present generation is postmortem. They have lived with the possibility of the death of all civilization and so they have developed a kind of gaiety or abandon, an attitude of what is there to lose?

Marcuse: They have seen daily the painful contrast between what is actually being done with the available resources of the human community and what might be done. Seeing all the barbarism, repression, exploitation, and injustice, they have lost the illusion that they live in a civilized society. So, once again, I don't see any need to look for hidden or mystical motives to account for the emergence of a militant youth.

Raser: Your remark about the possibility of the superpowers' getting together raises a question for me. Anatol Rapoport has argued that the main actors in the drama of human conflicts are no longer individuals but systems, superorganisms in which human beings play roughly the same role that the cell plays in the body. He calls these organisms *Stati Belligerens*—war-waging states. The most developed of these are Russia and the United States. These states are vast bureaucratic complexes with their own information receptors, data-processing centers, decision rules, communication networks, memory systems, and effectors. To these mechanical leviathans, private human passions are totally irrelevant.

Marcuse: If he makes no distinctions between these bureaucracies, then this is the type of generalization to which I must object. First, we are not informed about the direction China is going. And the Western world, capitalism, and Soviet socialism cannot really be thrown into the same boat because their *potential* development is so different.

Raser: But what about the lesser assertion that we have a growing kind of superorganism that is not responsive to the individual?

Marcuse: Yes, but why call it an organism? I cannot subscribe to the view that our social conflicts should be interpreted as battles between the individual and the superbeast. In my view there is a much simpler formulation—the established powers wage a concerted and organized fight against any attempt at revolution from below. And such revolutions are usually class efforts or group efforts rather than individual efforts.

Keen: This raises the crucial question about the whole category of the individual. Some radicals see the need to go beyond the notion of individual consciousness and to create a new form of tribal or communal consciousness. Would you say the concept of the individual is obsolete?

Marcuse: I wouldn't say the concept of the individual is obsolete. It is premature. The real human individual does not yet exist. What you have is a questionable bourgeois individual whose identity is based upon competitive performance against all other "individuals."

Keen: If the psyche of the quasi-individual of today is organized around the principles of performance and competition, what would be the organizing principles of a new revolutionary person? What would his sensibilities and rationality look like?

Marcuse: Let me first formulate it negatively because the negative contains the positive. It would be a psyche, a mind, an instinctual structure that could no longer tolerate aggression, domination, exploitation, ugliness, hypocrisy, or dehumanizing, routine performance. Positively you can see it as the growth of the esthetic and the erotic components in the instinctual and mental structure. I see it manifested today in the protest against the commercial violation of nature, against plastic beauty and real ugliness, against pseudovirility and brutal heroism.

Raser: When you talk about the instinctual structure of the new man are you implying a return to a more natural state? Is this a neo-romanticism?

Marcuse: Definitely not. I have been criticized for being against science and technology. This is utter nonsense. A decent human society can only be founded on the achievements of science and technology. The mere fact that in a free society all alienated labor must be reduced to a minimum presupposes a high degree of scientific and technical progress. The possibility of an esthetic, joyful transformation of the environment depends upon continuing technical advance. How can you speak of a return? This vision anticipates the future, it does not yearn for the past.

Raser: Well, among certain elements of the young there is today a real nostalgia for the simple, the primitive, the wilds, the animals. It seems to be based on a hatred of technology in all of its manifestations.

Marcuse: I would say it is a hatred of the present *abuses* of technology. I see nothing wrong with it; it does not entertain the notion of the noble savage. There is absolutely nothing wrong with establishing a libidinal relationship with nature; in fact, I think it is part of the liberation of man. But on the social scale there can never be a recurrence of a previous stage which existed only in mythology and poetry.

Keen: One of your friends told me of luring you to Montana for a lecture with the promise that he would show you wild mountain sheep. I take it that somewhere in your vision of Utopia there must be a wild place?

Marcuse: Yes, but not too wild. We don't want animals who eat each other and eat humans. We must not ignore the fact that nature is by no means gentle. It is just as cruel as the human reality. That is why I insist that the liberation of man involves the liberation and reconciliation of nature.

Raser: "The wolf also shall dwell with the lamb, and the leopard shall lie down with the kid; and the calf and the young lion and the fatling together . . ."

Marcuse: My allergy against the Scriptures is not such that I must say a priori that every single thing in the Scriptures is reactionary and repressive.

Keen: What would the reconciliation between man and nature look like?

Marcuse: Negatively, it would mean stopping the ruthless violation and destruction of nature. The ecological movement is beginning to spell out how this might be done. Already there is a consciousness of the damage this pollution of nature is doing to man. But the ecological movement must seek not the mere beautification of the existing Establishment but a radical transformation of the very institutions and enterprises which waste our resources and pollute the earth. They must be abolished and replaced by ones that drastically reduce pollution to an absolute minimum.

Raser: You think some pollution is inevitable then?

Marcuse: I don't know. That is a question for honest scientists and technologists. But I want to make clear what I mean by undoing the violation of nature. There is general agreement that an essential transformation of the environment and the humanization of life would imply the dissolution of the present cities and the creation of an architecture that reestablishes harmony between human habitation and the surrounding natural environment, as was the case in medieval towns in Europe where you still have the feeling of a symbiosis between man and nature. I don't see any reason why such a goal on a much higher level cannot be attained today. Certainly the automobile would have to be replaced as the chief means of transportation; noise and massive togetherness would have to be eliminated; population growth would have to be reduced. Instead of bulldozers tearing out trees and flattening the landscape they could follow the outlines of hills and valleys and respect the existing vegetation. So it doesn't mean the renunciation of machines, but a more sensitive use of them.

Raser: As you are talking I am reminded of Norman O. Brown's idea of putting rational thought and technology underground and letting poetry and madness play on the surface. You sound sympathetic to this notion.

Marcuse: I do. But don't they already play on the surface? My difference with my friend Norman Brown is that in my view he is too mystical and escapist, particularly in his last book, *Love's Body*. He wants to abolish things which I am very much interested in retaining. For instance, if I understand his mysticism correctly, it includes abolition of the distinction between male and female and creation of an androgynous person. He seems to see the distinction between male and female as the product of repression. I do not. It is the last difference I want to see abolished.

Keen: But Brown's language is so metaphorical it is hard to know whether he is advocating an end to genital sexuality or merely an end to the obsession with genital sexuality. I see a great similarity between your talk about new sensibilities and his idea that erotic consciousness involves breaking down the boundaries of the world through poetry —for instance, the boundaries between the body and the body politic.

Marcuse: But my basic objection is on political grounds. I want my concept of sensibility to be understood as a revolutionary concept, while *Love's Body* lives and takes refuge in a mystical universe.

Keen: I understand the difference between you and Brown in this way: when he talks about the body becoming erotic, he is advocating wordplay and poetic vision. Therefore, he uses the word "body" metaphorically. When you speak of new sensibilities, you are talking about a new relationship between the actual body and the body politic.

Marcuse: That's right. The eroticized body would rebel against exploitation, competition, false virility, conquest of space and violation of nature—all the established conditions. In this context we can say that the seeds of revolution lie in the emancipation of the senses [Marx]—but only when the senses become practical, productive forces in changing reality.

Keen: Then the real limitations to the development of sensibility are first in the community and only then in the psyche?

Marcuse: No. I would have to say it the other way around. You will be able to establish an authentic community only if it consists of human beings who have this new sensibility.

Raser: It seems like a closed circle to me.

Marcuse: Why?

Raser: If the structure of our psyche, that form of our consciousness, is so determined by the nature of the society in which we live, I can't understand how you can have transformation of the individual without the transformation of society and vice versa.

Marcuse: I can't see it clearly either. But as we discussed before, you can be determined by your community and the determination can be a *negative* one.

Keen: So you may be determined to fight that which is determining you.

Marcuse: Yes.

Raser: Speaking about people who seem to be determined to resist the conditions that violate them, would you like to say anything about Angela Davis?

Marcuse: Well, I can only say what I have said before. Angela was my best student, or one of my three or four best students. She certainly has demonstrated beyond the shadow of a doubt that she is not only highly intelligent but also a highly sensitive human being. And if you were to ask me how she came to involve herself in this Soledad kidnapping and killing, my first reaction would be that as far as I know it is the highest principle of Anglo-Saxon law to consider a person innocent unless his or her guilt has been proven in a court of law. No such proof has been given. What do we actually know of her role in this affair? I suppose we know that two or three or four guns were bought and registered in her name. Is that enough to pass judgment? These guns were reportedly used in the kidnapping. Do we know whether she even knew about it? Do we know how and for what purpose she gave the guns away if she did give them away? We don't know any of that. Angela became active in black politics only relatively recently. While she was at Brandeis and until 1965 she was practically nonpolitical. Then she went to Frankfurt am Main for two years, and when she came to La Jolla in 1967 she became involved immediately in the black movement. I don't find anything contradictory in a person of an unusually high level of intelligence and sensitivity and becoming directly active in politics. Angela was brought up in Alabama and had experienced in her own mind, and probably in her own body, all the deprivations of the black people there. It was perfectly natural for her to become active in politics.

Raser: On a more general level how do you feel about the increasing turn toward violence on the part of the young militants, black and white?

Marcuse: As you probably know, I make a distinction between violence and counterviolence. The violence of aggression is different from the violence of defense not only in its means and goals but in the instinctual structure out of which it grows. If somebody assails you on the street you instinctively react with all possible defensive violence at your disposal. This is certainly quite different from the violence of shooting into a crowd or tear-gassing a demonstration. Let me say further, there are acts of violence by pseudopolitical radicals that I think are stupid, criminal, and only play into the hands of the Establishment.

Raser: Such as kidnapping and bombing?

Marcuse: I don't want to single out specific instances and groups. I leave it to your imagination which ones I mean. Terror has been effective historically only if the terrorizing groups are already in power. Think, for example, of the Jacobin terror during the French Revolution. That was terror exercised by the group holding power, not by a group fighting for it. Groups trying to gain power have never been able to use terror effectively for any length of time. Look at the anarchists and nihilists in Russia. It didn't help one bit.

Raser: You said a moment ago that you see defensive and aggressive violence growing out of different instinctual or psychic structures. Would you elaborate on that?

Marcuse: Let me state the matter in Freudian terms. The balance between the aggressive instinct and the life instinct is different in the two forms of violence. In offensive violence the aggressive component has practically subdued the erotic. In defensive violence it is the other way around. I admit that this is very speculative and abstract but it seems to make sense. There is the familiar example of the sublimation of aggressive instincts in the interests of the life instincts in Freud's interpretation of the surgeon. The surgeon's primary aggressiveness is sublimated by placing it in the service of the preservation of life.

In our society as a whole we have not succeeded in sublimating these aggressive instincts. They are rampant in a way that is unprecedented in the world. This is perhaps the most violent society that has existed in civilization. That is why we need the concept of the death instinct to explain what is going on. Unlike the Romans, the Medici, the Huns, or other societies characterized by high levels of interpersonal violence, in America violence is managed, manipulated, and steered from above. It seems ingrained in the social institutions and relationships.

Keen: There seems to be a fine dividing line between violence and competitiveness. The Dutch historian Johan Huizinga in his classic book *Homo Ludens* says that the essence of play is the contest, or the *agon*. Can you conceive of a man in whom all violence, all competition was eradicated, a non-agonal man?

Marcuse: Certainly not. I cannot imagine a human society without what you call the agonal component. I don't think you can or ought to eliminate it because it brings great benefits. I can, for example, well envisage creative competition in refining and improving life on earth.

Raser: You don't think competition has an internal logic that leads it to escalate toward destructive violence?

Marcuse: No. I am afraid I am a terrible optimist. I realize that it does so today—that competition escalates toward violence—but if we can transform society this need not be the case.

Keen: Your thought has been subject to repeated attack from both the Right and the Left. Would you like to beat your critics to the punch with any self-criticism?

Marcuse: Yes, I must say about myself that I have probably emphasized unduly the most extreme and radical goals of the revolution-to-be. And I did not see to what extent we are already in the midst of what I call a preventive counterrevolution in which the established society is using all possible mental and physical means to suppress the radical opposition. So the heroic period of the militant student opposition is over. You see the heroic period was that of the hippies and Yippies. They did their thing. They did an indispensable job. They were heroes. They probably still are, but we have moved into a different period, a higher period in terms of historical sequence. We are now in the midst of the organized counterrevolution. You cannot have fun with fascism. What is required is a wholesale reexamination of the strategy of the movement.

Keen: So perhaps the strategy of confrontation politics is not appropriate in this stage?

Marcuse: That depends on what you mean by confrontation. The forms of confrontation are already changing. Take, for example, the case of the university. The sit-in, the occupation of buildings, and other forms of protest will now be met with legal action. The authorities will get injunctions, take the demonstrators to court, and sentence them to jail or heavy fines. This will finish many of the protesters for years. So it is becoming increasingly costly to use forms of confrontation which were still possible a year ago. Everyone in the movement has to reflect and think out what forms of effective confrontation and organization are still open to them in this period of counterrevolution.

Raser: Do you have ideas of possible directions?

Marcuse: That should be left to the movement. You know that I have always rejected the role of a father or grandfather of the movement. I am not its spiritual adviser. And I have enough confidence in the active and authentic students to believe that they can do that by themselves. They don't need me.

Man & Myth

A CONVERSATION WITH JOSEPH CAMPBELL

Campbell Joseph, educator, author: b. N.Y.C. Mar. 26, 1904; grad. Canterbury Sch., 1921; A.B. Columbia 1925, M.A. 1927; student U. Paris 1927–28, U. Munich 1928–9; m. Jean Erdman May 5, 1938; Tchr. Canterbury Sch. 1932–3; mem. faculty lit. dept. Sarah Lawrence Coll. 1934—; Pres. Creative Film Found. 1954–63; trustee Bollingen Found. 1960–9; Mem. Soc. for Arts, Religion and Contemporary Culture (dir.). Author: *The Hero with a Thousand Faces* 1949; *Masks of God, Vol. I: Primitive Mythology* 1959; *Vol. II: Oriental Mythology* 1962; *Vol. III: Occidental Mythology* 1964; *Vol. IV: Creative Mythology* 1967; *The Flight of the Wild Gander* 1969. Editor: *The Viking Portable Arabian Nights* 1952; *Papers from the Eranos Yearbooks (Vols. 1–6)* 1954, 55, 57, 61, 64, 68. Contr. articles profl. publs. Office: Sarah Lawrence Coll. Bronxville, N.Y. 10708.

The man and his work are a study in counterpoint. He sits, straight-spined, on a backless bench in an office walled round with books. Faded Navaho rugs cover the floors; icons and pictures of gods and heroes peer out from behind stacks of papers. In this quiet place, a scarce block from the cacophony of Washington Square in lower Manhattan, the maverick scholar has worked for thirty-five years to produce the books that have made him the foremost modern expert on mythology. In this oasis of order he has written of the hero who must venture into uncharted chaos in search of meaning. Campbell's scholarly quest into the mythologies of the world culminated in his four-volume series,

69

The Masks of God, which is the nearest thing we have to a modern version of Sir James George Frazer's *Golden Bough.*

Campbell's fascination with myth was born the day Buffalo Bill brought his Wild West show to Madison Square Garden. To a wide-eyed little boy in New York City, the collection of fierce Plains Indians, authentic survivors of the battle of Wounded Knee, were adventure, excitement and mystery all rolled into one. The show was indeed mythical—Wounded Knee was more massacre than battle—and it lured Campbell to the Museum of Natural History and to the public library. By the time he was eleven he had graduated from Lewis Henry Morgan's *League of the Iroquois* to the reports of the Bureau of American Ethnology. Soon he began to notice parallels between the Indian *myths* and the stories of creation, floods, virgin birth, resurrections that were the *truths* of the Roman Catholic Church he attended. Perhaps it was then that he formulated his least serious definition of myth: myth is other people's religion. At least he began to suspect that there were common themes in the stories of diverse peoples.

At Columbia University Campbell studied cultural history, managed to become one of the top half-milers in the country, and played saxophone in a jazz band. After a postgraduate year studying the Arthurian romances he received a traveling fellowship and spent a year at the University of Paris and a year at the University of Munich studying Sanskrit, Oriental philosophy, and religion. In Paris Campbell began to read Freud, Jung, James Joyce, and Thomas Mann. Again the parallels struck him. He began to suspect that the unconscious dreams and the conscious art of modern man contained the same themes he had found earlier in Indian myths. He returned to America in the beginning of the Depression. Living on the money he had earned playing jazz in college, he spent the next five years studying and looking for the universals of the mythical imagination.

The synthesis Campbell had been searching for emerged in his study of the hero and resulted in his most widely known book, *The Hero with A Thousand Faces.* This book took mythology out of the library and placed it at the center of the modern quest for identity. Behind the thousand faces of ancient and modern heroes Campbell discovered a single human quest, a standard pattern. Modernity does not essentially change the repertoire of human possibilities. As Campbell says, "The latest incarnation of Oedipus, the continued romance of Beauty and the Beast, stand this afternoon on the corner of 42nd Street and Fifth Avenue, waiting for the traffic light to change." Thus myths can no longer be dismissed as obsolete stories of a prescientific mentality. We live the same story as Jesus or Prometheus. We must, in Jung's words, "dream the myth onward," repeating perennial human themes in a manner that is colored by our individuality.

The counterpoint between the uniqueness of the individual and the available repertoire of psychic possibilities is a major theme of Campbell's thought. In 1954, after thirty years of being so immersed in Eastern art, philosophy, and religion that he considered himself "almost a Hindu," Campbell traveled to India. And the gods played apple-basket-turnover. He was so appalled by the caste system and by the lack of respect for the individual that he returned a confirmed Westerner, celebrating the uniqueness of the person.

It is little wonder that Campbell should emerge from his studies in mythology with conclusions that are more conservative than radical. When it comes to the primal scripts by which the human psyche is structured, there is little new under the sun. Nor is it surprising that Campbell, observing the radical rhetoric that warms Washington Square with each returning spring, should say that radicals always claim that times are about to change— that their ideas have gained momentum to achieve escape velocity and then end up stuck in the same orbit, returning every year to the same point in space. No doubt this hard saying is anathema to the liberal mind that always believes in the redemptive promise of the tomorrow that lies just beyond modernity. Perhaps it is not a counsel of despair but an invitation to embrace the abiding human condition. Only those modest enough to face the ineradicable limits of human energy and time may find the courage of the hero.

Sam Keen: Once upon a primal time, in the milk-soft youth of the race, every man's birthright of personal identity gave him a full share in corporate legends, rituals and myths. Psychology was a minor branch of the art of storytelling and myth-making. Now, in the modern secular mind, myths are the outdated illusions of prescientific people. What is a myth? And have we really passed beyond mythological thinking into the full light of reason?

Joseph Campbell: Let's begin by trying to untangle the confused notion of myth. In the past, the mythological system of any tribe or culture has served four functions:

First, the mystical or metaphysical function of linking up regular waking consciousness with the vast mystery and wonder of the universe. Any part can be a symbol for the whole. For instance, for Dante, Beatrice's beauty leads to the realization of divine love as the moving power of the universe.

Second, the cosmological function of presenting some intelligible image or picture of nature. In primitive cultures the relationship between man and woman is frequently seen as a mirror of nature: the universe is created by a union of Father Sky and Mother Earth.

Third, the sociological function of validating and enforcing a specific social and moral order. The example that comes to mind is the Ten Commandments and the Deuteronomic Law which were believed to have been revealed directly to Moses by God.

And finally, the psychological function of providing a marked pathway to carry the individual through the stages of life: the dependency of childhood, the responsibility of adulthood, the wisdom of old age, and the ultimate crisis of death. Every culture has rites of passage and related myths that serve this need.

Keen: But myths no longer do these jobs in modern culture. We allow normal waking consciousness and the sense of the mystery of the universe to exist in schizophrenic isolation because we no longer trust metaphysical or religious symbols. We take our cosmology from science and our morality from custom.

As for a vision of the stages of life, Americans of this particular day and age, at least, seem to make only one division between an extended period of youth and an ignored period of decrepitude and age. What place is left for mythology to occupy?

Campbell: I don't think there can ever be a general, comprehensive mythology. For there to be a shared mythology there must be a shared body of experiences. In small, horizon-bound societies everyone was immersed in the same social and visual reality. So if everyone lived with cattle or sheep, pastoral images were common. But our contemporary world is so heterogeneous that few people share the same experiences. Pluralism makes a unifying myth impossible. But if we cannot reinstate such a mythology we can, at least, return to the source from which mythology springs: the creative imagination.

Keen: In other words, a journey into the unconscious is now necessary to find the meanings and comforts that myths once gave us?

Campbell: Yes. After all, the myths originally came out of the individual's own dream consciousness. Within each person there is what Jung called a collective unconscious. We are not only individuals with our unconscious intentions related to a specific social environment. We are also representatives of the species *homo sapiens.* And that universality is in us whether we know it or not. We penetrate to this level by getting in touch with dreams, fantasies, and traditional myths; by using active imagination.

Keen: In a pluralistic culture, then, every individual must create a private mythological system. I must discover within myself the Garden of Eden from which I am exiled and the New Jerusalem toward which I am journeying. And must bear the burden of being my own redeemer, my own Christ.

Campbell: That is the essential meaning of the journey of the hero, which I consider the pivotal myth that unites the spiritual adventure of ancient heroes with the modern search for meaning. As always, the hero must venture forth from the world of commonsense consciousness into a region of supernatural wonder. There he encounters fabulous forces—demons and angels, dragons and helping spirits. After a fierce battle, he wins a decisive victory over the powers of darkness. Then he returns from his mysterious adventure with the gift of knowledge or fire, which he bestows on his fellow man.

Whenever the social structuring of the unconscious is dissolved, the individual has to take a heroic journey and go within to find new forms. The biblical tradition, which provided the structuring myth for Western culture, is largely ineffective. Its pretensions to revelation are refuted. So there must be a new quest. The same thing happened to the American Indians when the buffalo became extinct. They went in for the peyote cult and found new gods.

Keen: Are LSD and pot a part of the spiritual technology that the modern hero may use to get quick access to the mythological depths?

Campbell: I think drugs have uncovered the unconscious depths in a society that is lopsidedly rational and evaluative. They have shown many people that the archetypes are in the unconscious. They are as real as tables and chairs. But the drug culture has been caught in the fuzzy end of things—astrology, Kabala, Tarot, witchcraft, divination, and the like—as well as in a more serious encounter with the religious myths and practices of the East—Zen, meditation, yoga, etc. But there has been too much violence and frenzy in all of this. The young seem bewildered by the world of the psyche. They came into it too fast. It is like the situation in Greek mythology in which a person says to a god, "Show me yourself in your full power." And the god does and the person is blown to bits.

Keen: What is the alternative?

Campbell: I prefer the gradual path—the way of study. My feeling is that mythic forms reveal themselves gradually in the course of your life if you know what they are and how to pay attention to their emergence. My own initiation into the mythical depths of the unconscious has been through the mind, through the books that surround me in this library. I have recognized in my quest all the stages of the hero's journey. I had my calls to adventure, guides, demons, and illuminations. In the conflict between the Celtic-Arthurian and the Roman Catholic myths, I discovered much about the tensions that shaped my past. I also studied primitive myths and Hinduism and later Joyce, Mann, Jung, Spengler, and Frobenius. These have been my major teachers.

Keen: Why leave out Freud, the major guide to the unconscious?

Campbell: Freud was important for me for a while. But I don't think he is a good guide to mythology. He shows the way mythology becomes pathological. For instance, when a person is hysterical or neurotic he reads mythological symbols only in terms of his limited personal fix. Freud's basic mistake was in trying to extend the situation of the infantile crisis and family romance to provide an interpretation of the totality of culture. The basic myths that have supported historical cultures do not represent a regression of the race to childhood patterns; they are an aid in opening the human spirit to infinite domains of possibility and fulfillment.

Keen: In other words, the dynamics of the Oedipus complex describe only the repressive authoritarian family and cannot be used to understand the political problem of the relation of authority and repression?

Campbell: Exactly. Freud made the same mistake of historicizing myth that was made in the Bible, in the Judeo-Christian tradition. The Bible talked about the childhood of the Hebrew race; all of its mythology was grounded in the pseudohistorical events of Israel. In the same way, Freud found the formative principles of personality in the pseudoevents of childhood—in the Oedipal drama—and later in his theory of the primal horde. He projected this pattern onto society as a whole.

Keen: I wonder if it isn't the tragic myth rather than the family romance between Father, Mother, and little Lord Oedipus that determined Freud's thought. He saw an inevitable tragic conflict between the Dionysian forces of the id and the Apollonian structures of the ego. Pleasure and reality, nature and society, Eros and Thanatos are joined in endless warfare. He did not, for instance, see the possibility you write about in *The Hero With a Thousand Faces*—that the hero may descend into the underworld of the id and be reborn in a way that resolves the conflict between desire and duty.

Campbell: In order to understand Freud, it is important to see the way his thought, although it is highly secularized, arose out of his Jewish heritage. His psychology was uniquely Jewish.

This is one of the big problems in world mythology. Why is it that Semitic people—and this goes for the old Acadians, the Babylonians, and the Amorites as well as the Jews—place their tribal deity at the top of their mythology? No other people did this. Other cultures recognize the nature divinities as the great powers and the tribal deities as inferior. The main thing about the Jewish myth was that it had no trust in nature. In the Old Testament, Yahweh was in perpetual conflict with the fertility cults and the nature goddesses. In cultures dominated by nature deities you could go from one locality to another and say, "The deity whom you call Neptune we call Poseidon, and so we have the same gods." But when the tribe experienced the tribal god and his rules as the incarnation of the holy, they established a situation of social and theological exclusiveness.

Keen: The accidents of history, the idiosyncratic experience and morality of the tribe, then became the determining form of religion and of the psyche.

Campbell: Right. Look at the Jewish festivals. They were the same festivals everybody else celebrates, but they were made to refer to pseudoevents in Jewish history. Passover was the resurrection of Adonis. Chanukah was the birth of the Sun. When the Jews historicized these myths they lost contact with the world of nature.

Now, the psychic counterpart of the world of nature is the collective unconscious. Let me translate: we share the same gods—we are informed by the same archetypes. The natural forces that animate us are common and divine.

Freud's suspicion of the instinctual forces of the id, and his assumption that they must be shaped and controlled by the ego, was a reflection of the animosity between Yahweh and the goddesses of nature. Everyone in the Freudian tradition—and this includes existentialists like Sartre—is afraid of nature. To them, nature is absurd. It causes nausea.

But nature is not so chaotic. Energy comes to us already inflected, specified, and organized. You can't call nature absurd simply because it does not fit into the Cartesian coordinates, because it can't be reduced to a system of clear and distinct ideas. Its order is marvelous although it frequently escapes the narrow categories of our reason.

Keen: If traditional religious mythology is no longer believable, and Freud is little better, what guides do we have for our descent into the unconscious? Is it the case, as R. D. Laing suggests, that we have lost even the small comfort former generations had of having names for the demons and spirits that inhabit the void? Are we to refuse the trip to the depths or be abandoned in the maze with no thread of Ariadne to lead us out?

Campbell: Perhaps. Perhaps the artist is the best prototype of the modern hero. James Joyce or Thomas Mann, for instance, have created a new mythology. Jung also provides some notion of the stock characters that have played in the dreams and myths of all mankind. These archetypes still inform the unconscious and provide a standard repertoire of mythic fantasies. But each individual will experience the archetype—of the anima, or the shadow, or the wise old man—in a unique manner. Only the form of the archetype is set. The content is taken from individual experience. So, the modern hero who must venture into the underworld of the unconscious has some maps to help him on the journey.

Keen: If the artist becomes the new guide, then the task of creating myth is no longer a communal undertaking.

Campbell: That is precisely the problem of modern man. In traditional societies the symbols and myths that were the vehicles of social values were presented in socially maintained rites that the individual was required to experience. All the meaning was in the group, none in the self-expressive individual. Today the situation is reversed. The creative mythology of the modern artist arises when the individual has an experience of his own—of order, or horror, or beauty—that he tries to communicate by creating a private mythology. So it is the creative individual who must give us a totally new type of nontheological revelation, who must be the new spiritual guide.

Keen: In the position you are stating, the artist becomes the new messiah. His lonely, self-conscious odyssey gives modern man his only map for the journey toward liberation. There is an elitist assumption, implicit in your view, about the redeeming function of art. How are the nonliterary to find an identity? Is the quest of the alienated intellectual the model for the way all modern men must discover meaning?

Campbell: I think we have to distinguish between three different types of persons and paths of creativity. The traditional myths—Christian and otherwise—still offer support for large numbers of people in our society. And there is a mode of creative life that exists within the horizons of known and accepted values. For example, bringing up a family is a good and honest lifework that gives meaning and satisfaction. It is a different, but not lower, form of creativity from that of the artist. Then there is the path of the scientist whose quest is directed toward the exterior world of nature. A third type is the individual who is forced to undertake an inner quest because neither the accepted myths nor the outward path is satisfying. The quester is the person who has failed; he has cracked up; he has run into the interior difficulties that have made it necessary for him to reorganize his life on a higher level than that of the person who hasn't cracked up. So the work of the artist is in some ways a response to necessity. Something happens to him and he has to respond or disintegrate. In all the myths of adventure the hero starts out innocently looking for something lost or following an animal into the forest, and before he knows it he is in a place nobody has ever been before that is filled with monsters or demons that may destroy him. Creative artistic work is a response to the need to escape from this danger and chaos and find some new security.

Keen: I notice you say the quest leads to an integration on a higher level than is achieved by the person who remains within the culturally accepted patterns. The artist and adventurer are, then, elite.

Campbell: Of course. Why deny it? Our culture, like all cultures, requires elites. Without elites there would be no literature, science, or even creative entertainment. A culture without dreams is finished. It has nothing to motivate it. There is also a way in which the notion of an elite is not limited to the intellectual classes. Anybody who has any competence on any level belongs to an elite. Generally, human beings are proud of what they can do well, whether it is writing a book or building a house or seducing girls. Any action well-done tends to generate an elite appreciation. People even become elite slobs and pride themselves in being able to go a little further into the abyss than anybody they know.

Keen: You uphold and celebrate the individual. A lot of people seem to be experiencing disillusionment with individualism. The new search for community—the emergence of communes, collectives, and group-living arrangements—suggests that for many persons the Western romance with the individual is finished. Can there be no communal adventure, no path toward novelty and integration, that is shared?

Campbell: Let me answer with an incident from the Arthurian myths that has been central for me. King Arthur would never allow the knights of the round table to begin a meal until an adventure had occurred, and of course, in those wonderful days, an adventure would always occur. In this particular incident the Grail, covered by a satin cloth, appeared in midair in the hall and then disappeared. Sir Gawain, Arthur's nephew, stood up and proposed that all should go forth upon a quest to discover the unveiled Grail. After Mass they were to depart. And here is the line that inspired me: "They thought it would be a disgrace to go forth in a group." Then each entered the forest at the point that he had chosen, where it was darkest and there was no way or path because (now I am interpreting) where there is a path it is someone else's path. This epitomizes for me the quality of Western man that is gorgeous. Every individual is a unique phenomenon and the task of life is to bring this uniqueness to fruition. This accounts for the strange quality of yearning in the Occident. What does Western man yearn for? We yearn for something that never was on land or sea—namely, the fulfillment of that intelligible character that only the unique individual can bring forth. This is what Schopenhauer called "earned character." You bring forth what is potential within you and no one else.

Keen: Are you suggesting that personality is an invention of Western culture?

Campbell: In the Orient the path of salvation is to follow a way that already has been marked out by the guru. You go to a guru with perfect faith and no questions. He didn't question his guru, and so on. So, theoretically at least, the pure light of antique wisdom comes down unmodified by the creative impulses of the individual. Personality must be erased in order for truth to emerge. The goal of Oriental mysticism is to wipe out the ego. Incidentally, I think there is a confusion in Eastern thought between ego and id. They interpret the ego as saying "I want, I possess," but it is the id that is the source of desire. When you get rid of desire and yearning what remains is nothing: Nirvana. And that is the goal of the East, not yearning and personality.

Keen: You seem to see an opposition between the individual and the community, insight and tradition, adventure and initiation.

Campbell: Nothing so absolute. But I think a person's courage to live should not be confined to the courage to be with a certain group. This philosophy, which is cropping up again in the communes, sets up a therapeutic community as an ideal. There are times when people need therapeutic communities, but they should not be confused with rich life—a therapeutic house is not a home.

Keen: Do you see groups as agencies for specific action? Isn't it possible, for instance, for twenty or fifty persons to arrive at the same conclusion, to reach the same place in the forest and join in a common search for the Grail?

Campbell: Yes. But the group is the agent for actions that have been decided by individuals. The individual is to the group as the quest for the Grail is to the organized Church. In the Arthurian legends the Grail appears only to the person who is ready for it, who is spiritually eligible for the vision. In the Church there are leaders who tell the followers what to think and how to worship. The priests hear confessions, celebrate the Mass, and assure the faithful that salvation is theirs. The adventurer must always quest for the Grail, man alone. By definition you can't bring the crowd along. After the adventure the hero can teach the crowd, if he chooses.

In the myths of Christ and the Buddha there is a very interesting point. In the Buddha legends, Ananda is the Buddha's favorite body servant and a person of charming character. Saint Peter plays the same role in the Christ legend. Ananda never got things quite right. Neither did Peter. Christ says at one time, "Peter, you do not understand spiritual things. I will make you head of my church." The Buddha says to Ananda, "Why can't you get things straight? I will make you the head of my church." The leaders of the crowd are necessary people. But they don't get things quite right.

Keen: Can you be less metaphorical about the quest? If the group cannot provide norms, how is the individual to know whether he is on the right way?

Campbell: To find your own way is to follow your own bliss. This involves analysis, watching yourself and seeing where the real deep bliss is—not the quick little excitement, but the real, deep, life-filling bliss. My way has been the way of bliss in reading. I will not finish a book that bores me, no matter how important it is. This has been my discipline. As a result, I have left unread a lot of things I ought to have read, and I have read many things I ought not to have read. It is not respectable to admit it, but I have read everything Frobenius ever wrote.

Keen: I would like to probe a little deeper into social transformation. The myth of the hero concerns the process in which the individual grows by descending to the depths, being torn apart, and then ascending to a fuller life. There seems to be a direct parallel between this myth and the apocalytic myth of Marcuse and the New Left, which says the whole society must suffer upheaval, death, and rebirth. Must we have social revolution before the individual can find health?

Campbell: I don't believe in the dismemberment of society as a whole. I have been sitting here at the corner of Waverly Place and Sixth Avenue, a stone's-throw from Washington Square, for thirty-odd years, and I have heard every soapbox orator the changing social conditions have produced. And it is always the same story. It has been one experience of my life that times have always been just about to change and nothing ever happened. The same thing is just about to happen all the time. The current dogma, which is also widespread in the university, is the Marxist idea of the necessity for total revolution. I disagree with Marx, and also with R. D. Laing, when they say you cannot have a harmonized psyche until you have a harmonized society. The whole nature of life has always been one of struggle and destruction and rebirth. There is no such thing as an ideal society, and to wait for it before you can make yourself whole seems to me absurd. I think the Buddhist doctrine that all life is sorrowful is the beginning of wisdom. It does away with the illusion that there will be, in some indeterminate future, an unsorrowful, unambiguous, utopian form of life.

Keen: Then all apocalyptic thought discourages us from accepting the abiding ambivalence of actual life? Marcuse, no less than the heaven of Christian theology, distracts us—with the promise of a saccharine future—away from the bittersweet present.

Campbell: Right. Apocalypse is basically rooted in hatred. Think of the apocalypse of the biblical writers, how they hated everybody —the Assyrians, the Babylonians, the Greeks, the Romans.

One of the finest students I have taught in recent years asked me the other day, "Have you ever hated life?" I thought back and tried to recall some time that I could possibly have hated life. And I said,

"No, I don't honestly think I ever have, and I don't see how I ever could." "Well," she said, "You are the only intellectual I know who doesn't." I thought of the crowd she was going with and they were all involved in the social leftist line, which means that the world as it is is no good and you can't live unless it gets a lot better. This mood seems to dominate the university today. And what a destruction of human joy it has created!

It is always the day after tomorrow that is going to be good.

Keen: Apocalyptic thought conceives that perfection, harmony, and the absence of conflict are necessary conditions for happiness. Since these are absent in the actual society of the moment, revolution is necessary to create a new order that will be discontinuous with the present impure society. You seem to stand opposed to this manner of thinking. Your work suggests that we need a mythology that will allow us to value continuity and celebrate the world as we find it. You want us to be at home in the imperfections of the present moment.

Campbell: Above all we need to be taught more affection for the infirmities of life. Intellectuals too often denigrate the existing order in deference to some possible utopia.

Keen: Is it possible to teach such an affection?

Campbell: I think so. Thomas Mann gives us a clue in the notion of erotic irony that he develops in the story Tonio Kröger. Tonio is a sensitive youth who has lost his way in the world. He recognizes the beauty, charm, and worthiness of the life of the simple citizen, but it does not satisfy him. So he goes to Bohemia, which was the Hippieville of those days.

There he falls in with intellectuals. They are critical of the whole world of normal life, yet they don't seem to make it as active, vital human beings. So Tonio is doubly disillusioned, and he comes to the formula that is his rescue: the world of the artist or intellectual must be fierce and accurate in its judgment of the fault in a person or a society. But alongside this judgment there must be affirmation and compassion. What is important is to keep the dissonance between judgment and compassion.

Both artist and lover know that perfection is not lovable. It is the clumsiness of a fault that makes a person lovable.

Keen: If we are most authentically human when we are able to perceive and love all that is faulted, lame, and imperfect, then both education and therapy should beware of the rhetoric of triumph—becoming whole, realizing the full human potential, producing the man for all seasons.

Campbell: That is what interests me in Jung's method of therapy, which was designed to amplify rather than reduce the fault in the patient. Dreams reveal the repressed side of personality with all its strengths and weaknesses. Balance comes as a result of leaning on your faults. This is also a common theme in the folklore of the *Arabian Nights:* where you stumble and fall, there you find the gold.

Keen: Contemporary culture seems to be inundated with new heroes and quasimythological events: Hobbits and gurus, Beatles and Easy Riders, Woodstock Nations and moon walks. It is hard to distinguish between plastic events created by the media and the genuine-walnut-folk-crafted-hand-rubbed myths. What heroes and events seem to you to symbolize modern man's self understanding?

Campbell: The astronauts are the heroes and the moon walk the event that I find most significant.

Let's look at the symbolic significance of the moon landing. Before Copernicus, man's images of the cosmos corresponded to what was visible. The sun rose and set and the earth was obviously the center of the cosmos. Then Copernicus created a theory that removed earth from the center and placed it as one planet among many in the heavens. Although this theory has been intellectually convincing, it lacked the emotional impact of a cosmological image that was visible. You couldn't experience the new world view. Now, suddenly, through the eyes of the astronauts and the marvels of technology, we can stand on the moon and watch the earth rise over the lunar horizon. When we watch the rising earth we are able to see, for the first time, that the earth is in the heavens.

Now, let me take this one step further. In the ancient world—in fact right up until modern times—there has been a dichotomy between earth and heaven, matter and spirit, the realm of men and the sphere of the gods. And, of course, the stars in the heavens were considered divine. Now the earth has been elevated symbolically into the heavens, matter has been spiritualized. In a strange way, the moon walk has a symbolic significance parallel to the Pope's declaration of the bodily Assumption of the Virgin Mary (which Jung considered the most important theological statement of the twentieth century). Mother Earth is elevated to the dignity of the Father, the Son, and the Holy Ghost.

Keen: How does this reflect modern man's view of himself?

Campbell: It is the visible symbol that there is no longer a spiritual order external to man. Galileo demonstrated that the mechanical laws of the heavens were identical with those of the earth. Then Kant showed us that the forms of space and time were built into the human perceptual apparatus. And now NASA has given us empirical proof that the only world we can experience is conditioned by the mathematics of space. So the old dichotomy between the spirit and matter, God and man, is finished.

Keen: So man, who was once a child of the cosmos—dust inspired by spirit—has come of age and claimed for himself the creative power that formerly belonged to the gods.

Campbell: Yes, and if you look at the mandalas, the visible designs that symbolized world views, which have been characteristic of different ages, you can trace the progression of human self-consciousness. When man was a hunter, he considered the animals divine and he wore animal masks, created animal totems, and took animal names to signify his accord with the world around him. In agricultural societies the cycle of the seasons, the process of death and rebirth, became central. Later the mathematical pace of the planets moving through the fixed constellations became the center of wonder and man projected the gods in the form of solar deities who wore the crown of the sun. Still later, the Christian symbol of the cross became the center of the mandala. Now as Jung noticed in the mandalas of his patients, the human figure has become the focal point. Mankind—I and thou—must now create the world.

What gods are there that are not from man's imagination? All the gods are within us.

Keen: How splendid. And how very lonely.

From Dolphins to LSD

A CONVERSATION WITH JOHN LILLY

Reprinted from PSYCHOLOGY TODAY Magazine, December, 1971.
Copyright © Ziff-Davis Publishing Company.

Scientists and mystics, like slide rules and leprechauns, usually are discreet enough to remain in their separate worlds. And that is why John Cunningham Lilly is a bit embarrassing. When an established neurphysiologist-biophysicist begins to talk about levels of satori and takes up altering states of consciousness we don't know what to do with him.

There were signs and portents from the beginning that Lilly would not be satisfied with the myopia that keeps a timid scientist from focusing beyond his knows. He entered the world forty minutes after Alan Watts was born on January 6, 1915—evidently a vintage year for seers. While he was still in prep school he announced his intention to unite the microcosm and macrocosm; it was in his first "scientific" paper, modestly entitled "Reality." His central preoccupations then, as now, were: What is the relation of brain and mind? How does the internal world of experience relate to external reality?

Having rejected his inherited Catholicism, Lilly set out to investigate reality by the methods of consensus science. At the California Institute of Technology he studied physics, biology, and Freud and found he would have to go to medical school to pursue his interest in the brain and mind. After medical school at the University of Pennsylvania, he went to the E. R. Johnson Foundation of Medical Physics to continue his research in bio- and neuro-physics. In his spare time he underwent a training

89

analysis and attended the Institute of the Philadelphia Association for Psychoanalysis and became a qualified psychoanalyst. In 1953 he moved to Washington to the National Institute of Neurological Diseases and Blindness and NIMH, where he worked with monkey, rabbit, and cat brains. He mapped the spread of electrical activity in the cerebral cortex and studied motor and motivational systems in the cortex and subcortex.

In 1954, in an experiment to determine what happened to the brain when it was deprived of environmental stimuli, Lilly began to immerse himself in the dark world of water. Floating free and weightless, he observed the workings of his own mind. He watched cherished beliefs, assumptions, and concepts dissolve and form again under the calm gaze of his inner eye. He finally discovered the maxim that has been his sole guide for exploring inner space: every belief is a limit to be examined and transcended.

While he was immersed in the tank, Lilly began to wonder what goes on in the mind of an animal that has a brain as large as man's and lives constantly in water. After preliminary studies on dolphin brains, Lilly decided that the best way to get an answer was to ask a dolphin. In 1959 he established the Communication Research Institute in St. Thomas in the Virgin Islands and began an audacious attempt to establish interspecies communication. He has reported the results of this experiment in *Man and Dolphin* and *The Mind of the Dolphin*. Some think he succeeded too well. He became convinced that dolphins had sensibilities equivalent to those of human beings and that, therefore, he had no moral right to keep them in an experimental concentration camp for his scientific convenience. So he closed down the institute and set the dolphins free.

In 1969 Lilly plunged into the new world of the human-potential movement. While he was a resident at Esalen he heard tales of a master in Chile, Oscar Ichazo, who taught a modern version of ancient Sufi discipline for altering consciousness and achieving enlightenment. Lilly went to look and stayed to become a member of Ichazo's Arica training group. He plans to work with this group when it establishes a school in New York to teach Americans to reach the different levels of satori.

Lilly is something of an upside-down Maslow. He sees no need to settle for occasional peak experiences. A proper marriage of modern technology to ancient, esoteric techniques for achieving enlightenment—meditation, yoga, etc.—will allow the average person to live in the heights in an almost constant state of satori.

It is a startling vision for a scientist. But he is not alone. Consciousness III, or something like it, does seem to be emerging. At the very least, we know we can no longer tolerate the cultural schizophrenia that has severed fact from value, knowledge from wisdom, science from religion. If calculation is not rejoined to enchantment there may soon be no world to study or enjoy. Perhaps John Lilly provides some crucial guidelines that will help us remain grounded in what he calls "the planetside trip" and still soar into the outer galaxies of the mind. The world might be safer if we could get leprechauns and slide rules together. It certainly would be more fun.

Sam Keen: If there is a cartographer of altered states of consciousness—of the highways and byways of the inner trip—it is John Lilly. You are indeed a rare combination of scientist and mystic. You have traveled from the natural sciences to the esoteric sciences. You seem to incarnate the dissatisfaction that many moderns feel with the narrowly scientific way of knowing and being in the world. But many people still think of you first as the man who communicates with dolphins, so perhaps this is a good place to begin your story. How did you get into dolphin research?

John Lilly: There were several motivating interests. I had been working in brain and mind research for many years. In 1954 I began work in physical isolation in a water-filled tank. While floating around in the tank, I began to wonder about the mind of an animal who lived in water all the time and had a brain the size of man's. I knew the dolphin had a cerebral cortex as large as a human's. What was going on in that brain? Some people argued that a large body required a large brain. But there was the example of the whale shark who weighed forty tons and had a brain the size of a macaque monkey. So I began to ask, what is the dolphin doing with all that excess brain? When I began to study dolphin sounds I found they had an immensely more complex communication system than we do. This led me to question whether we might establish interspecies communication. If this could be done it would show us what the human mind has in common with other creatures with large brains. This knowledge, in turn, might prove valuable if our space program should detect nonhuman, intelligent beings outside the earth.

Keen: What were the major problems you faced in communicating with dolphins?

Lilly: The first problem was attitude. The human species is so arrogant, it is difficult for us to entertain the idea that there may be superior beings swimming around in the sea. So we had to approach the dolphins with gentleness and respect and with the assumption that they had as much desire to communicate with us as we did with them.

Then there was the problem of the different structure of dolphin and human languages. Our vocal communication is airborne and is relatively slow. The dolphin sonic communication is waterborne and is thus about ten times faster than ours. This means the dolphin receives the bulk of his information about his environment acoustically, while we receive ours visually. The visual inputs in the dolphin are only one-tenth the capacity of our visual inputs, but their acoustical inputs are ten times greater than ours. So the total amount of information received by dolphins and humans from their environments is roughly the same. But the types differ. We are not going to understand dolphins adequately until we can translate their language to ours. We need to experience how they hear their world.

Keen: How did you establish communication with them?

Lilly: It began with an accident. One day in 1955 we were listening to a tape of dolphin sounds. We suddenly got the weird feeling that the dolphins were mimicking our speech. In fact, they were laughing at us. So, someone suggested that we go out and see if one of our young dolphins, Elvar, would copy a word. We went into the tank and I shouted at Elvar, "Water." He came up, put his blowhole in the air, and went, "Wa . . . ter," breaking the word in the middle. And so we started to work on the word "water," and within twenty minutes Elvar was copying it.

Later we set up a more intensive experiment in which a young woman, Margaret Howe, lived with and became teacher, friend, mother, and lover to a young male dolphin by the name of Peter. She taught him to reproduce simple words with humanoid sounds, to respond to greetings, to distinguish objects, to say the names of numbered balls, and to respond to elaborate directions. In time they developed genuine verbal and nonverbal communication. Margaret Howe would say, "Peter, go get the orange ball." There might be five balls all of different colors floating on the water. Peter would go and bring back the blue ball, the green ball, etc. Every one but the orange ball. An operant conditioner observing Peter might conclude that he didn't understand what we were saying. But Margaret would say, "He knows damn well what I mean because he brought me the orange ball five times in a row yesterday on command."

Keen: If you can break the rules in a creative way it means you must understand the rules.

Lilly: Right. A pigeon might peck the right button five times, but a dolphin won't. He is too smart and having too much fun. He changes the rules of the game because he is intelligent enough to get bored with oversimple games. He is trying to get a message across to you. You just can't do the operant-conditioning game with someone who is really intelligent and insists on having a good time. If you want to examine the intelligence of a superior being you have to be willing to observe him on his terms.

Keen: Some critics suggest that neutral researchers cannot replicate your results. How do you answer this?

Lilly: The basic question at issue here is the status of the scientific observer: Who is watching what under what conditions with what assumptions? If we are going to test the hypothesis that dolphins have intelligence equal to or superior to human beings, we have to be willing to adopt the perspective of the dolphins. Treat a dolphin like a stupid animal and that is all you will observe. The operant conditioner is sitting back as an omniscient observer judging the animal and expecting certain reproducible behavior. If he doesn't get that behavior he considers the animal stupid. He doesn't think to ask a new question, as one does with an intelligent human.

Keen: A scientific observer must be willing to be changed by the object he is investigating.

Lilly: Yes. There is always continuous feedback between the observer and the system he is observing. The observer must always simultaneously be building a model of the system he is observing and of the observer. John van Neuman and Leo Szilard showed this for quantum mechanics. To do quantum mechanics correctly, you have to have the quantum observer who goes down into the system to be observed, and he has to follow certain laws of observation depending on the system. When he comes back into the Newtonian universe with its large assemblages of matter, he must become a Newtonian observer. And when he goes up near the velocity of light, he has to become an Einsteinian observer. So, when you start observing dolphins, you have to become a dolphin observer. A dolphin observer is not, by definition, an operant conditioner. He must be sensitive, respectful, and involved with his (hypothetically) superior animals in an ethical way.

Keen: Why did you stop working with dolphins?

Lilly: In 1964 I built an eight-foot tank, filled it with sea water and began my work with LSD and physical isolation. The dolphins were in the same lab and I began to see the ethical implications of my beliefs about dolphins. If what I believed about dolphins was true, I had no right to hold them in a concentration camp for my scientific convenience. So I decided to end the project. On the day I arrived at this decision, but before I had told any of my colleagues, my favorite dolphin decided to commit suicide.

Keen: How does a dolphin commit suicide?

Lilly: Sissy just stopped eating. We gave her animal enzymes to stimulate her appetite and got her going for a while. But she finally decided to hell with it and stopped breathing. We had her for seven years, since she was nine months old, and she liked us better than she liked dolphins. After this, five more dolphins committed suicide within two weeks. So I told everyone about my decision, and we turned the three remaining dolphins loose.

Keen: Do you intend to do any further research with dolphins?

Lilly: If I could get the right conditions. I would have to have a wet house by the sea designed so the dolphins could come and go at will. Then I would like to have a family with young children that could learn to play and communicate with young dolphins. I think only such a long-range, free project will allow us to take the next step in interspecies communication.

Keen: I would like to go back to your research on the effects of LSD and physical isolation. Was this connected with your dolphin work?

Lilly: No. I began the experiments with physical isolation when I was with NIMH in Washington. In neurophysiology there has long been a question of what keeps the brain going. Where are its energy sources? One obvious answer was that the energy sources are strictly biological and internal and they do not depend on the outside environment. But some people were arguing that if you cut off all the stimuli to the brain it would go to sleep. So we decided to test this hypothesis. This was easily done by creating an environment in a tank that would isolate a person from external stimuli. For a couple of years I periodically immersed myself in the tank and studied my states of consciousness. During this time I did not use LSD. Many of my colleagues at NIMH were working with it but I did not want to prejudice my observations about the psychedelic spaces I was getting into in the tank.

Keen: What happens to your body when you are in a stimulus-free environment?

Lilly: You can forget your body and concentrate on the workings of your mind. But if any stimulus remains it becomes overwhelming.

Once when I was in the tank a series of bubbles formed from the water and began to hit my foot. As each bubble traveled up my leg I experienced an exquisite pleasure. In fact, the pleasure was so great that it turned to pain when the bubbles began to come at about five-second intervals.

Keen: Were the effects of physical isolation comparable to those you later discovered in using LSD?

Lilly: The effects are similar. It is possible in the tank for the person who knows how to relax, to *park his body,* to go into any of the psychelic spaces without using LSD. Only the energy level differs. LSD allows you to jack the energy level way up. Physical, mental, and spiritual energy runs higher.

Keen: It is difficult to believe that physical isolation produces such dramatic changes. Do you need elaborate training or a special facility to get to psychedelic levels of consciousness without drugs?

Lilly: Certainly it is easier to reach a level of consciousness or psychic space once you have been there before. But all the average person has to do is get into the tank in the darkness and silence and float around until he realizes he is programming everything that is happening inside his head. You are free of the physical world at that point, and anything can happen inside your head, because everything is governed by the laws of thought rather than the laws of the external world. So you can go to the limits of your conceptions.

Keen: Your imagination is totally free?

Lilly: Well, I don't like the word "imagination." When you are in the tank you are certain of the reality of what you are experiencing. I started off with the notion that I was creating everything I experienced. But a lot of things happened that made me ask some radical questions about the nature of reality and different modes of perception. I began then to see that interpreting all the novel experiences in the tank as projections was an arrogant assumption.

Keen: What kinds of experiences did you find difficult to interpret in commonsense terms?

Lilly: I went through an experience in which another person I knew apparently joined me in the dark, silent environment of the tank. I could actually see, feel, and hear her. At other times I apparently tuned in on networks of communication from other civilizations in other galaxies. I experienced *parking* my body and traveling to different places.

Keen: This could well sound like a report from a first-class schizophrenic. What kept you from interpreting these experiences as evidence of psychosis?

Lilly: I think the attempt to define all mystical, transcendental, and ecstatic experiences which do not fit in with the categories of consensus reality as *psychotic* is conceptually limiting and comes from a timidity which is not seemly for the honest, open-minded explorer. Also, I knew something about the world of psychotics. I had a complete training analysis with Robert Walder and had a speaking acquaintance with my own psychotic spaces, and I had worked with catatonic and schizophrenic patients. It was not psychosis I was exploring in the tank, but belief structures. I was examining the way in which we program our beliefs and impose limits on what we may perceive and experience by these beliefs. I wanted to know what principles were governing the human mind. If we consider the human mind as a kind of computer, I was looking for the basic programs which were built into the computer and the meta-programs which we impose upon the mind by conscious choice or unconscious compulsion. And I wanted to discover how many of the meta-programs could be raised to the conscious level and be changed or reprogrammed.

Keen: Did you discover any essential rules that can serve as guides to the explorer of inner space?

Lilly: After ten years in the tank I formulated a working rule: whatever one believes to be true either is true or becomes true in one's own mind, within limits to be determined experimentally and experientially. These limits themselves are, in turn, beliefs to be transcended. The limits of one's beliefs set the boundaries for possible experience. So every time you reach a limiting belief it must be examined and gone beyond. For the explorer there are no final *true* beliefs.

Compulsion is being trapped in a *known* psychic reality, a dead-end space. Freedom is in the unknown. If you believe there is an unknown everywhere—in your own body, in your relationships with other people, in political institutions, in the universe—then you have maximum freedom. If you can examine old beliefs and realize they are limits to be overcome and can also realize you don't have to have a belief about something you don't yet know anything about, you are free.

Keen: Did you develop specific techniques in the tank for examining your limiting beliefs?

Lilly: Yes. I have just written a book, *The Center of the Cyclone,* that deals with the rules for exploring the inner-outer spaces of consciousness. The basic skill is one that has been known since ancient times. In yoga and in Eastern thought it has been called establishing the fair witness or the witnessing self. I think of it as becoming an observer and watching the operation of the programs which are governing your thinking and behavior. You can pull out of an experience, step back, and watch the program. Much of psychoanalysis involves gaining this skill of seeing how you have gotten trapped in the past with some program that solved a problem in childhood but that was overgeneralized and carried forward and has continued to operate in inappropriate situations. Tremendous energy is locked up in these old programs or what Jung called "autonomous complexes." You can release this energy if you get enough distance from your emotional involvement in the programs to see them like an old movie on T.V. or like a tape loop that you have heard a thousand times. As soon as you get distance you realize you are not the programmer, and you are not that which is programmed, and you are not the program. Your identity becomes established as an independent agent. Once this ability to disidentify yourself from old programs, programming, and from the programmer becomes generalized, you have the key to higher states of consciousness. By refusing to identify with the programs, you transcend them and gain a measure of control. In this way you begin to exercise the meta-programming powers of the human bio-computer, the ability to create self-consciously the principles that govern thought and behavior.

Keen: Does the fair-witness technique work for dealing with present experience and future expectations as well as for examining compulsive patterns we have carried over from the past?

Lilly: Of course. Premature judgment and closure is the greatest danger for the person who wants to retain the psychic mobility of the explorer. A good general rule for dealing with situations where you are overwhelmed with novelty is: when you are in a new space where you can't account for what is happening on the basis of past assumptions, stay wide open and let your fair witness store all the information you receive. Later on you can slow down and play it all back without editing and can evaluate what has happened to you.

It is at least an ideal aim to be free of unexamined programs which govern thought and behavior. In Eastern thought this was what was meant by being free of karma. The fair witness is able to function without the imposition of limiting patterns from past experience. I have sometimes described this as the goal of making the human bio-computer general-purpose. In this sense I mean that in the general-purpose computer there can be no display, no acting, no ideal that is unavailable to consciousness. This is also near to what Freud meant by the aim of making the unconscious conscious. There should be no boundaries within the computer.

Keen: You describe continuous iconoclasm that is intoxicating and frightening. I can smell the wind blowing across the vast open spaces, but I am not certain it is possible to live in an attitude of continuous exploration. Every time a system of beliefs breaks down or is transcended, the result is chaos and anxiety. Social and psychological limits and boundaries are erected to keep chaos and anxiety within tolerable quantities.

Lilly: No! This is a perfect example of what we have been talking about. And once you recognize it you don't have to follow it. You don't have to suffer continual chaos in order to grow. That is the old

Christian program—you can't have heaven without hell; you can't have a cosmos without chaos. This is what I call the trampoline effect.

Keen: You seem to be challenging one of the more deeply held principles of identity that has governed the Western psyche. I think of Dostoevsky's vision: man knows the angel in himself only to the extent that he converses with his devil. Or of Freud's notion that ego is strong only to the degree that it has integrated the underworld of the id. There is no ascension into heaven without a descent into hell, no resurrection without crucifixion, no success without failure, etc. This rhythm or oscillation has been central to the Western notion of growth.

Lilly: I am not denying the existence of a duality or plurality in man. I only say that simultaneity rather than oscillation is a better, more economical way of dealing with this duality. You don't have to keep going down in order to go up.

Once you know any "negative" system such as fear exists, you can get the energy out of it by rising above it through meditation and observation.

Keen: There is a growing interest here in psychological disciplines and philosophy of the East. Meditation and yoga are almost as common today as prayer meetings were a generation ago. How did you get into mysticism?

Lilly: I left the Catholic Church when I was thirteen, when I decided that the whole mystical thing—God, angels, afterlife—was all childish nonsense. I went full speed into science. But when I began my work with physical isolation, I began to experience a super-self level, a network of interrelated essences. Your essence, my essence, everybody's essence are hooked together. And there is immediate and total communication with them all the time throughout the whole galaxy.

Keen: Is this your way of rendering the experience out of which the classical notion grew that man is a microcosm of the macrocosm, that his reason or *logos* partakes of the reason or *logos* that informs all of reality?

Lilly: Yes. But that classical idea never made any sense to me until I experienced the network of intelligences, the galactic or universal network or what was called Universal Mind in idealistic philosophy and Eastern religion.

In 1964, as the result of an accident, I went through a death experience. I was in a coma for twenty-four hours and was blind for two days after that. In the coma I entered a space I hadn't been in since I was twenty-two, when I had four wisdom teeth pulled under gas. I had also been in the same space at age seven when my tonsils were taken out, and when I was five and had t.b. Each time I had almost died, or thought I was going to die, two characters or guides kept turning up. Every time I have a job to do, these characters show up and tell me what the job is.

In the tank in the Virgin Islands I tried to get back to the place where I had met the guides by using LSD without the fear of death. In spite of some fear, I relaxed, and I was immediately in their space. The two guides began to come toward me from a vast distance. As they approached their presences became powerful and I noticed their thinking, feeling, and knowledge pouring into me. Just as I felt I would be overwhelmed by their presence, they stopped. As they stopped, in effect they said, "We will not approach any closer as this seems to be your limit at this time. You can come back here any time once you have learned the routes. We are sent to instruct you. So far you have been doing your experiments in solitude and have learned some of the ways to get here. Now you should contact others like yourself who have these capacities, help them, and learn from them. Perfect your means of communicating with this level, but stay in your body. There are other methods than LSD plus solitude for achieving these results."

After these initial contacts I began to feel the presence of my guides without going into their spaces.

Keen: Does it now seem to you that these guides are more than poetic projections of your own imagination?

Lilly: The two guides may be aspects of my own functioning at the super-self level. They may be helpful constructs, or concepts. They may be representatives of an esoteric hidden school. They may be members of a civilization a hundred, a thousand years or so, ahead of ours. Or I may be tuning in on networks of communication of a civilization beyond ours which is radiating information throughout the galaxy. I don't know.

Keen: Much of your work with physical isolation and LSD seems to be an effort to establish a set of disciplines for dealing with kinds of experiences which a scientistic culture has considered paranormal or even abnormal. Are we now developing practices that will allow us some orderly access to altered states of consciousness?

Lilly: We are approaching a marriage between the modern scientific point of view and the old esoteric and mystical knowledge. Now we are exploring new modes of access to states of consciousness which have been experienced for centuries. It is an empirical approach to those dimensions of consciousness that Eastern thinkers spoke of as levels of enlightenment or satori. I want to elaborate a series of maps and some rules of the road.

Keen: What kinds of maps have you developed for the outer spaces of human consciousness?

Lilly: The most helpful one for me was developed by Oscar Ichazo, the master who runs the school in Chile in which I have spent the last eight months. He uses the analogy of the length and frequency of sound waves to characterize the different levels of consciousness. Level 48 is the rational, neutral state. At this level your mind is operating efficiently but without emotion. This is the type of consciousness in which the head tripper lives most of the time. The experiences of different types of satori, or enlightenment, begin at level 24. Level 24 involves enjoyment in doing some activity that is done well and without conflict. This is the professional satori, the state of integrated work. As we move up in the psychedelic scale to level 12, we reach a state of blissful awareness. At level 12 you can't function smoothly in the world because you are in bliss. You still are in your body, but the reality around you seems alive. This is the first level of a good LSD trip. At this level it is frequently difficult to speak. You accept the here and now. Sometimes this state can be reached in sexual intercourse. It is also the kind of enlightenment Zen speaks about. At level 6 you get out of your body for the first time. You become a point of consciousness, love, energy, warmth, cognition. This point is mobile. It can travel inside your body or into outer spaces. You still have your own I, your center of consciousness, but your body is not experienced.

At level 3, the highest level of satori from which people return, the point of consciousness becomes a surface or a solid which extends throughout the whole known universe. This used to be called fusion with the Universal Mind or God. In more modern terms you have done a mathematical transformation in which your center of consciousness has ceased to be a traveling point and has become a surface or solid of consciousness. Here you lose the I almost completely, although you do retain some memory of this state when you come back. It was in this state that I experienced "myself" as melded and intertwined with hundreds of billions of other beings in a thin sheet of consciousness that is distributed around the galaxy.

Keen: If a person has this map available, can he learn to get into these states of consciousness without using drugs?

Lilly: Yes, drugs may help in the sense that they give some awareness of the existence of different modes and levels of consciousness. Gradually a tolerance is building up in regard to marijuana and LSD, a new kind of permissiveness about all means for the alteration of consciousness. But once you know a space exists you can learn to get back to it. You can program yourself to move into any space you know exists if you use discipline and concentration.

This is the most turned-on country the world has ever seen. The rest of the world is way behind. Our kids are turned on to levels of consciousness and possibilities of travel into mental and spiritual spaces in an unprecedented way.

Keen: Do you think the consciousness revolution will eventually change the way technology is used?

From Dolphins to LSD   **103**

Lilly: It will improve it immensely.

Keen: The exploration of inner space is producing a body of new knowledge. Who will disseminate it, and to whom?

Lilly: I see it being transmitted to and within the Establishment. The new exploration of consciousness is a way of life. You will be seeing it on television and in the other media. Already the younger generation is sharing its knowledge of how to alter awareness.

But the people I am most interested in are the successful heads of corporations and bureaucracies. Many of these people already operate at the level of satori 24. They are joyfully locked into their work. But they have never had maps which suggested to them the possibility of achieving more blissful levels of consciousness.

What might happen if they could visualize the possibility of spending the weekend in satori 12, or even of achieving satori 3, in which they would realize that their essences are hooked to every other essence in the whole universe?

Keen: A touch of mystical madness might unite us to nonhuman forms of consciousness—we might even begin to feel a kinship with other members of our own species.

Lilly: It might turn out that exploring the far-out spaces of human consciousness is the fastest way to social transformation.

Sorcerer's Apprentice

A CONVERSATION WITH CARLOS CASTANEDA

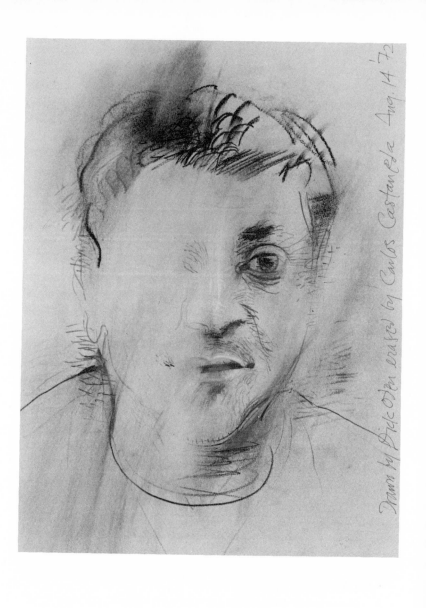

Drawn by Professor erased by Carlos Castaneda Aug. 14 '72

Sorcerers are not fond of statistics, verifiable knowledge, or established identities. Their tradition is ancient, their knowledge is esoteric, and their way of life is surpassing strange. When Carlos Castaneda began to report on the teachings of don Juan he was more than a spectator to the world of sorcery but something less than a convert. In subsequent years he found the wisdom of don Juan to be the most certain guide on "the path with heart." He is more elusive as a disciple than he was as an anthropologist. The more notoriety his books gain, the farther he retreats from public attention. His books, *The Teachings of Don Juan, A Separate Reality,* and *Journey to Ixtlan,* have sold half a million copies.

To compensate for his growing image and legend, Carlos Castaneda erases his personal history and deliberately withholds information that would destroy the anonymity he needs so that he can wander freely in whatever worlds there are or may be. When he is caught in the official world, where withholding autobiographical information is tantamount to treason, he may give his name, rank, and serial number. Then, like the Lone Ranger, he disappears in a cloud of rumor.

Usually reliable sources report that Castaneda was born in Brazil thirty-three or thirty-four years ago. He spent most of his early life in Argentina before he came to the United States to study anthropology. In the summer of 1960 he set out to gather information on medicinal plants.

He met and became a friend of an old Indian—don Juan Matus —who was reputed to know something about peyote. After a year of slow-growing friendship, don Juan explained that he was a *brujo* (sorcerer, medicine man, or healer) and had decided to pass along his secret knowledge to Carlos. Castaneda accepted, confident of his ability to rationalize and transcend the weird world of sorcery and keep his anthropological cool. For the next twelve years Castaneda commuted between the halls of the University of California at Los Angeles and the haunted hills of Mexico. While he played on the margins of madness he managed to retain his sanity and to work on a Ph.D. in anthropology.

More interesting than the putative facts about Castaneda are the transformations he has undergone and the marvels he has witnessed. Once he became a crow. With only a little help from the smoke of a magical plant, he watched crow's wings sprout from what had been his cheekbones and a tail grow from his neck. And then he flew off with three other crows on a three-day trip. (Anyone who has ever hunted crows would envy anyone who had a chance to crawl inside their uncanny heads. As experts in carrion—sanitation engineers—they must be able to distinguish between the living and the dead. This makes them experts in motion. Their wisdom consists in the ability to tell when things are moving too fast, too slow, and just right. And that is no mean knowledge. It might serve well in our culture in which we worship a demon god called Progress who keeps us moving and changing at an insane rate.)

And that is only the beginning. In the course of his apprenticeship Castaneda encountered creatures seldom found this side of the looking glass. When he tried to enter the separate reality of the sorcerer's world he was stopped by a gnat that was close to 100 feet tall. There were other dangers. A beautiful sorceress, la Catalina, tried to steal his soul and forced him into deadly combat. Once he almost killed her with a shotgun when she made the mistake of assuming the form of a blackbird and flying too near don Juan's house. When Carlos finally summoned sufficient nerve to ram a wild boar's hoof into la Catalina's navel, she saw that his intent was strong and she ceased to bug him. Much of Carlos' power came from his meeting with Mescalito, the strawberry-headed, green-skinned spirit of peyote. But there were times when he saw unbelievable things without even a little help from his psychotropic friends. One day don Juan and his friend don Genaro made Carlos' car disappear before his stone-sober eyes. And there was the time he had a conversation with a luminous, bilingual coyote.

All of these are but minor tricks, occasional far-out trips. The marvel of marvels was Castaneda's steady journey to the heart of ordinary reality. Things are seldom what they seem. In sharing the sources of his sorcery, don Juan sought to develop in Carlos the ability to see the everyday world with wondering eyes. Don Juan is a good sociologist of knowledge. He knows that the world of commonsense reality is a product of a social consensus. To marvel we need to strip ourselves of the explanations and assumptions that shape and limit our vision. If we bracket our normal ways of perceiving the world, we can see how arbitrary they are. Don Juan used sorcery and psychotropic plants to help Carlos in this process of bracketing. The most sophisticated philosophers of our century have tried to accomplish the same thing by pure thought or intellection.

Here fiction and fact entwine to turn event into allegory. A student of the German phenomenologist Edmund Husserl, knowing of Castaneda's interest in phenomenology, gave him a piece of ebony that once sat on Husserl's writing desk. Carlos had read and discussed passages of Husserl's *Ideas* with don Juan and passed the gift on to him. Don Juan fondled the ebony, as Husserl had done a generation before, and gave it an honored place in his treasury of power objects that are used for conjuring. And it is wholly appropriate. Husserl sought to escape from the subjectivity and solipsism that was the legacy of Descartes' definition of man as a rational being enclosed within the certainties of his own mind. Don Juan likewise taught that it is a mistake to get caught in the world of the psyche and neglect the marvels that are all around us. There is no salvation or sanity to be found within the isolated self. If we can discover ways of deconditioning consciousness, of erasing the barriers to perception that are imposed on us by common sense, there is no telling what strange things we may discover. There are certainly more things under heaven than philosophers or psychologists or stockbrokers imagine.

In his most recent book, *Journey to Ixtlan,* Castaneda shows that it was more the realistic than the fantastic aspects of don Juan's teachings that convinced him that there was no other way to live an exuberant life. "Don Juan kept reminding me that I had to die," he says. When death became a reality for Castaneda he was able to change, to become more decisive, and to be less governed by the expectations of others and by ordinary social routines. He accepted the ideal of the life of the warrior who must discipline his body and accumulate personal power. By experiment with living impeccably Carlos discovered the paradoxical unity of opposites. Discipline and abandon, realism and fantasy, secondary- and primary-process thinking go hand in hand. There need be no enmity between sanity and ecstasy.

Every age discovers or creates the heroes it needs. Ours has a strange bunch. Perhaps we feel that we are increasingly strangers in a strange land and so we populate our new world with Hobbits and gurus, charismatics and explorers of altered states of consciousness. The names of Carlos Castaneda, don Juan, Timothy Leary, John Lilly, and other psychonauts are known to many persons who think that Neil Armstrong is the all-American boy who used to be on the radio just before "Terry and the Pirates." Our occult heroes testify to the desire for a new age of enchantment. We have become disenchanted with the old dreams. We thought accumulated wealth would bring us security, and that technological power would allow us to manipulate the environment until it satisfied our every wish. We have found as much anxiety as happiness and more chaos than progress. Now it seems to be time to try another way. Neither technology nor government can change the world sufficiently to satisfy the needs of persons who understand eventually that they must die. So we revive the ancient notion of the power of personal vision. The new mysticism proclaims that enlightenment must take precedence over projects for social change. The eye of the beholder must be purified before it can see new possibilities. There is danger in enchantment. We know that the tyrannical dominion of machines, profit, and power politics will bring only increasing alienation and injustice. But it does not follow that a retreat from politics into nature mysticism or privatism will serve the cause of survival. Vision without politics is as dangerous as politics without vision. We need the disconcerting marvels of don Juan's world no less than we need the prophetic protests of the Berrigans. And we all might borrow crows' eyes and take a hard look at our rate and direction of movement. When Castaneda returned from his flight with the crows he was shaken for many days. He lived with the anxiety common to all voyagers who enter the world on the other side of the looking glass. For a time he did not know whether he was a professor pretending to be a crow or a crow pretending to be a professor. Then he laughed and knew that literal truth and poetry can never be separated. What is important is to fly high and return to earth.

Sam Keen: As I followed don Juan through your three books, I suspected, at times, that he was the creation of Carlos Castaneda. He is almost too good to be true—a wise old Indian whose knowledge of human nature is superior to almost everybody's.

Carlos Castaneda: The idea that I concocted a person like don Juan is inconceivable. He is hardly the kind of figure my European intellectual tradition would have led me to invent. The truth is much stranger. I didn't create anything. I am only a reporter. I wasn't even prepared to make the changes in my life that my association with don Juan involved.

Keen: How and where did you meet don Juan and become his apprentice?

Castaneda: I was finishing my undergraduate study at UCLA and was planning to go to graduate school in anthropology. I was interested in becoming a professor and thought I might begin in the proper way by publishing a short paper on medicinal plants. I could have cared less about finding a weirdo like don Juan. I was in a bus depot in Arizona with a high-school friend of mine. He pointed out an old Indian man to me and said he knew about peyote and medicinal plants. I put on my best airs and introduced myself to don Juan and said: "I understand you know a great deal about peyote. I am one of the experts on peyote (I had read Weston La Barre's *The Peyote Cult*) and it might be worth your while to have lunch and talk with me." Well he just looked at me and my bravado melted. I was absolutely tongue-tied and numb. I was usually very aggressive and verbal, so it was a momentous affair to be silenced by a look. After that I began to visit him and about a year later he told me he had decided to pass on to me the knowledge of sorcery he had learned from his teacher.

Keen: Then don Juan is not an isolated phenomenon. Is there a community of sorcerers that shares a secret knowledge?

Castaneda: Certainly. I know three sorcerers and seven apprentices and there are many more. If you read the history of the Spanish conquest of Mexico, you will find that the Catholic inquisitors tried to stamp out sorcery because they considered it the work of the devil. It has been around for many hundreds of years. Most of the techniques don Juan taught me are very old.

Keen: Some of the techniques that sorcerers use are in wide use in other occult groups. Persons often use dreams to find lost articles, and they go on out-of-the-body journeys in their sleep. But when you told how don Juan and his friend don Genaro made your car disappear in broad daylight, I could only scratch my head. I know that a hypnotist can create the illusion of the presence or absence of an object. Do you think you were hypnotized?

Castaneda: Perhaps, something like that. But we have to begin by realizing, as don Juan says, that there is much more to the world than we usually acknowledge. Our normal expectations about reality are created by a social consensus. We are taught how to see and understand the world. The trick of socialization is to convince us that the descriptions we agree upon define the limits of the real world. What we call reality is only one way of seeing the world, a way that is supported by a social consensus.

Keen: Then a sorcerer, like a hypnotist, creates an alternative world by building up different expectations and manipulating cues to produce a social consensus.

Castaneda: Exactly. I have come to understand sorcery in terms of Talcott Parsons' idea of glosses. A gloss is a total system of perception and language. For instance, this room is a gloss. We have lumped together a series of isolated perceptions—floor, ceiling, window, lights, rugs, etc.—to make a single totality. But we had to be taught to put the world together in this way. A child reconnoiters the world with few preconceptions until he is taught to see things in a way that corresponds to the descriptions everybody agrees on. The world is an agreement. The system of glossing seems to be somewhat like walking. We have to learn to walk, but once we learn, there is only one way to walk. We have to learn to see and to talk, but once we learn, we are subject to the syntax of language and the mode of perception it contains.

Keen: So sorcery, like art, teaches a new system of glossing. When, for instance, Vincent van Gogh broke with artistic tradition and painted *The Starry Night* he was in effect saying: here is a new way of looking at things. Stars are alive and they whirl around in their energy field.

Castaneda: Partly. But there is a difference. An artist usually just rearranges the old glosses that are proper to his membership. Membership consists of being an expert in the innuendoes of meaning that are contained within a culture. For instance, my primary membership, like most educated Western men, was in the European intellectual world. You can't break out of one membership without being introduced into another. You can only rearrange the glosses.

Keen: Was don Juan resocializing you or desocializing you? Was he teaching you a new system of meanings or only a method of stripping off the old system so that you might see the world as a wondering child?

Castaneda: Don Juan and I disagree about this. I say he was reglossing me and he says he was deglossing me. By teaching me sorcery he gave me a new set of glosses, a new language and a new way of seeing the world. Once I read a bit of the linguistic philosophy of Ludwig Wittgenstein to don Juan and he laughed and said: "Your friend Wittgenstein tied the noose too tight around his neck so he can't go anywhere."

Keen: Wittgenstein is one of the few philosophers who would have understood don Juan. His notion that there are many different language games—science, politics, poetry, religion, metaphysics, each with its own syntax and rules—would have allowed him to understand sorcery as an alternative system of perception and meaning.

Castaneda: But don Juan thinks that what he calls seeing is apprehending the world without any interpretation; it is pure wondering perception. Sorcery is a means to this end. To break the certainty that the world is the way you have always been taught you must learn a new description of the world—sorcery—and then hold the old and the new together. Then you will see that neither description is final. At that moment you slip between the descriptions; you stop the world and see. You are left with wonder; the true wonder of seeing the world without interpretation.

Keen: Do you think it is possible to get beyond interpretation by using psychedelic drugs?

Castaneda: I don't think so. That is my quarrel with people like Timothy Leary. I think he was improvising from within his European membership and merely rearranging old glosses. I have never taken LSD, but what I gather from don Juan's teachings is that psychotropics are used to stop the flow of ordinary interpretations, to enhance the contradictions within the glosses, and to shatter certainty. But the drugs alone do not allow you to stop the world. To do that you need an alternative description of the world. That is why don Juan had to teach me sorcery.

Keen: There is an ordinary reality that we Western people are certain is *the* only world, and then there is the separate reality of the sorcerer. What are the essential differences between them?

Castaneda: In European membership the world is built largely from what the eyes report to the mind. In sorcery the total body is used as a perceptor. As Europeans we see a world out there and talk to ourselves about it. We are here and the world is there. Our eyes feed our reason and we have no direct knowledge of things. According to sorcery this burden on the eyes is unnecessary. We know with the total body.

Keen: Western man begins with the assumption that subject and object are separated. We're isolated from the world and have to cross some gap to get to it. For don Juan and the tradition of sorcery, the body is already in the world. We are united with the world, not alienated from it.

Castaneda: That's right. Sorcery has a different theory of embodiment. The problem in sorcery is to tune and trim your body to make it a good receptor. Europeans deal with their bodies as if they were objects. We fill them with alcohol, bad food, and anxiety. When something goes wrong we think germs have invaded the body from outside, and so we import some medicine to cure it. The disease is not a part of us. Don Juan doesn't believe that. For him disease is a disharmony between a man and his world. The body is an awareness and it must be treated impeccably.

Keen: This sounds similar to Norman O. Brown's idea that children, schizophrenics, and those with the divine madness of the Dionysian consciousness are aware of things and of other persons as extensions of their bodies. Don Juan suggests something of the kind when he says the man of knowledge has fibers of light that connect his solar plexus to the world.

Castaneda: My conversation with the coyote is a good illustration of the different theories of embodiment. When he came up to me I said: "Hi, little coyote. How are you doing?" And he answered back: "I am doing fine. How about you?" Now, I didn't hear these words in the normal way. But my body knew the coyote was saying something and I translated it into dialogue. As an intellectual my relation to dialogue is so profound that my body automatically translated into words the feeling that the animal was communicating with me. We always see the unknown in terms of the known.

Keen: When you are in that magical mode of consciousness in which coyotes speak and everything is fitting and luminous, it seems as if the whole world is alive and that human beings are in a communion that includes animals and plants. If we dropped our arrogant assumptions that we are the only comprehending and communicating form of life we might find all kinds of things talking to us.

John Lilly talked to dolphins. Perhaps we would feel less alienated if we could believe we were not the only intelligent life.

Castaneda: We might be able to talk to any animal. For don Juan and the other sorcerers there wasn't anything unusual about my conversation with the coyote. As a matter of fact they said I should have gotten a more reliable animal for a friend. Coyotes are tricksters and are not to be trusted.

Keen: What animals make better friends?

Castaneda: Snakes make stupendous friends.

Keen: I once had a conversation with a snake. One night I dreamt there was a snake in the attic of a house where I lived when I was a child. I took a stick and tried to kill it. In the morning I told the dream to a friend and she reminded me that it was not good to kill snakes, even if they were in the attic in a dream. She suggested that the next time a snake appeared in a dream I should feed it or do something to befriend it. About an hour later I was driving my motor scooter on a little-used road and there it was waiting for me: a four-foot snake, stretched out sunning itself. I drove alongside it and it didn't move. After we had looked at each other for a while I decided I should make some gesture to let him know I repented striking his brother in my dream. I reached over and touched his tail. He coiled up and indicated that I had rushed our intimacy. So I backed off and just looked. After about five minutes he went off into the bushes.

Castaneda: You didn't pick it up?

Keen: No.

Castaneda: It was a very good friend. A man can learn to call snakes. They sense everything, your activity and your feeling. But you have to be in very good shape, calm, collected—in a friendly mood, with no doubts or pending affairs.

Keen: My snake taught me that I had always had paranoid feelings about nature. I considered animals and snakes dangerous. After my meeting I could never kill another snake and it began to be more plausible to me that we might be in some kind of living nexus.

Our ecosystem might well include communication between different forms of life.

Castaneda: Don Juan has a very interesting theory about this. Plants, like animals, always affect you. He says that if you don't apologize to plants for picking them you are likely to get sick or have an accident.

Keen: The American Indians have similar beliefs about animals they killed. If you don't thank an animal for giving up his life so that you may live, his spirit may cause you trouble.

Castaneda: We have a commonality with all life. Something is altered every time we deliberately injure plant life or animal life. We take life in order to live, but we must be willing to give up our lives without resentment when it is our time. We are so important and take ourselves so seriously that we forget that the world is a great mystery that will teach us if we listen.

Keen: Perhaps psychotropic drugs momentarily wipe out the isolated ego and allow a mystical fusion with nature. Most cultures that have retained a sense of communion between man and nature also have made ceremonial use of psychedelic drugs. Were you using peyote when you talked with the coyote?

Castaneda: No. Nothing at all.

Keen: Was this experience more intense than similar experiences you had when don Juan gave you psychotropic plants?

Castaneda: Much more intense. Every time I took psychotropic plants I knew I had taken something and I could always question the validity of my experience. But when the coyote talked to me I had no defenses. I couldn't explain it away. I had really stopped the world and for a short time got completely outside my European system of glossing.

Keen: Do you think don Juan lives in this state of awareness most of the time?

Castaneda: Yes. He lives in magical time and occasionally comes into ordinary time. I live in ordinary time and occasionally dip into magical time.

Keen: Anyone who travels so far from the beaten paths of consensus must be very lonely.

Castaneda: I think so. Don Juan lives in an awesome world and he has left routine people far behind. Once when I was with don Juan and his friend don Genaro, I saw the loneliness they shared and their sadness at leaving behind the trappings and points of reference of ordinary society. I think don Juan turns his loneliness into art. He contains and controls the power, the wonder, and the loneliness, and turns them into art.

His art is the metaphorical way in which he lives. This is why his teachings have such a dramatic flavor and unity. He deliberately constructs his life and his manner of teaching.

Keen: For instance, when don Juan took you out into the hills to hunt animals was he consciously staging an allegory?

Castaneda: Yes. He had no interest in hunting for sport or to get meat. In the ten years I have known him don Juan has killed only four animals to my knowledge, and these only at times when he saw that their death was a gift to him in the same way his death would one day be a gift to something. Once we caught a rabbit in a trap we had set and don Juan thought I should kill it because its time was up. I was desperate because I had the sensation that I was the rabbit. I tried to free him but couldn't open the trap. So I stomped on the trap and accidentally broke the rabbit's neck. Don Juan had been trying to teach me that I must assume responsibility for being in this marvelous world. He leaned over and whispered in my ear: "I told you this rabbit had no more time to roam in this beautiful desert." He consciously set up the metaphor to teach me about the ways of the warrior. The warrior is a man who hunts and accumulates personal power. To do this he must develop patience and will and move deliberately through the world. Don Juan used the dramatic situation of actual hunting to teach me because he was addressing himself to my body.

Keen: In your most recent book, *Journey to Ixtlan,* you reverse the impression given in your first books that the use of psychotropic plants was the main method don Juan intended to use in teaching you about sorcery. How do you now understand the place of psychotropics in his teachings?

Castaneda: Don Juan used psychotropic plants only in the middle period of my apprenticeship because I was so stupid, sophisticated, and cocky. I held on to my description of the world as if it were the only truth. Psychotropics created a gap in my system of glosses. They destroyed my dogmatic certainty. But I paid a tremendous price. When the glue that held my world together was dissolved, my body was weakened and it took months to recuperate. I was anxious and functioned at a very low level.

Keen: Does don Juan regularly use psychotropic drugs to stop the world?

Castaneda: No. He can now stop it at will. He told me that for me to try to see without the aid of psychotropic plants would be useless. But if I behaved like a warrior and assumed responsibility, I would not need them; they would only weaken my body.

Keen: This must come as quite a shock to many of your admirers. You are something of a patron saint to the psychedelic revolution.

Castaneda: I do have a following and they have some strange ideas about me. I was walking to a lecture I was giving at California State, Long Beach, the other day and a guy who knew me pointed me out to a girl and said, "Hey, that is Castaneda." She didn't believe him because she had the idea that I must be very mystical. A friend has collected some of the stories that circulate about me. The consensus is that I have mystical feet.

Keen: Mystical feet?

Castaneda: Yes, that I walk barefooted like Jesus and have no callouses. I am supposed to be stoned most of the time. I have also committed suicide and died in several different places.

A college class of mine almost freaked out when I began to talk about phenomenology and membership and to explore perception and socialization. They wanted to be told to relax, turn on, and blow their minds. But to me understanding is important.

Keen: Rumors flourish in an information vacuum. We know something about don Juan but too little about Castaneda.

Castaneda: That is a deliberate part of the life of a warrior. To weasel in and out of different worlds you have to remain inconspicuous. The more you are known and identified, the more your freedom is curtailed. When people have definite ideas about who you are and how you will act, then you can't move. One of the earliest things don Juan taught me was that I must erase my personal history. If little by little you create a fog around yourself, then you will not be taken for granted, and you will have more room for change. That is the reason I avoid tape recordings when I lecture, and photographs.

Keen: Maybe we can be personal without being historical. You now minimize the importance of the psychedelic experience connected with your apprenticeship. And you don't seem to go around doing the kind of tricks you describe as the sorcerer's stock-in-trade. What are the elements of don Juan's teachings that are important for you? How have you been changed by them?

Castaneda: For me the ideas of being a warrior and a man of knowledge, with the eventual hope of being able to stop the world and see, have been most applicable. They have given me peace and confidence in my ability to control my life. At the time I met don Juan I had very little personal power. My life had been very erratic. I had come a long way from my birthplace in Brazil. Outwardly I was aggressive and cocky, but within I was indecisive and unsure of myself. I was always making excuses for myself. Don Juan once accused me of being a professional child because I was so full of self-pity. I felt like a leaf in the wind. Like most intellectuals, my back was against the wall. I had no place to go. I couldn't see any way of life that really excited me. I thought all I could do was make a mature adjustment to a life of boredom or find ever more complex forms of entertainment, such as the use of psychedelics and pot and sexual adventures. All of this was exaggerated by my habit of introspection. I was always looking within and talking to myself. The inner dialogue seldom stopped. Don Juan turned my eyes outward and taught me how to see the magnificence of the world and how to accumulate personal power.

I don't think there is any other way to live if one wants to be exuberant.

Keen: He seems to have hooked you with the old philosopher's trick of holding death before your eyes. I was struck with how classical don Juan's approach was. I heard echoes of Plato's idea that a philosopher must study death before he can gain any access to the real world and of Martin Heidegger's definition of man as being-toward-death.

Castaneda: Yes, but don Juan's approach has a strange twist because it comes from the tradition in sorcery that death is a physical presence that can be felt and seen. One of the glosses in sorcery is: death stands to your left. Death is an impartial judge who will speak truth to you and give you accurate advice. After all, death is in no hurry. He will get you tomorrow or next week or in fifty years. It makes no difference to him. The moment you remember you must eventually die you are cut down to the right size.

I think I haven't made this idea vivid enough. The gloss—"death to your left"—isn't an intellectual matter in sorcery; it is a perception. When your body is properly tuned to the world and you turn your eyes to your left, you can witness an extraordinary event, the shadow-like presence of death.

Keen: In the existential tradition, discussions of responsibility usually follow discussions of death.

Castaneda: Then don Juan is a good existentialist. When there is no way of knowing whether I have one more minute of life, I must live as if this is my last moment. Each act is the warrior's last battle.

So everything must be done impeccably. Nothing can be left pending. This idea has been very freeing for me. I don't have any more loose ends; nothing is waiting for me. I am here talking to you and I may never return to Los Angeles. But that wouldn't matter because I took care of everything before I came.

Keen: This world of death and decisiveness is a long way from psychedelic utopias in which the vision of endless time destroys the tragic quality of choice.

Castaneda: When death stands to your left, you must create your world by a series of decisions. There are no large or small decisions, only decisions that must be made now.

And there is no time for doubts or remorse. If I spend my time regretting what I did yesterday I avoid the decisions I need to make today.

Keen: How did don Juan teach you to be decisive?

Castaneda: He spoke to my body with his acts. My old way was to leave everything pending and never to decide anything. To me decisions were ugly. It seemed unfair for a sensitive man to have to decide. One day don Juan asked me: "Do you think you and I are equals?" I was a university student and an intellectual and he was an old Indian, but I condescended and said, "Of course we are equals." He said, "I don't think we are. I am a hunter and a warrior and you are a pimp. I am ready to sum up my life at any moment. Your feeble world of indecision and sadness is not equal to mine." Well, I was very insulted and would have left, but we were in the middle of the wilderness. So I sat down and got trapped in my own ego-involvement. I was going to wait until he decided to go home. After many hours I saw that don Juan would stay there forever if he had to. Why not? For a man with no pending business that is his power. I finally realized that this man was not like my father who would make twenty New Year's resolutions and cancel them all out. Don Juan's decisions were irrevocable as far as he was concerned. They could be canceled out only by other decisions. So I went over and touched him and he got up and we went home. The impact of that act was tremendous. It convinced me that the way of the warrior is an exuberant and powerful way to live.

Keen: It isn't the content of decision that is important so much as the act of being decisive.

Castaneda: That is what don Juan means by having a gesture. A gesture is a deliberate act which is undertaken for the power that comes from making a decision. For instance, if a warrior found a snake that was numb and cold, he might struggle to invent a way to take the snake to a warm place without being bitten. The warrior would make the gesture just for the hell of it. But he would perform it perfectly.

Keen: There seem to be many parallels between existential philosophy and don Juan's teachings. What you have said about decision and gesture suggests that don Juan, like Nietzsche or Sartre, believes that will rather than reason is the most fundamental faculty of man.

Castaneda: I think that's right. Let me speak for myself. What I want to do, and maybe I can accomplish it, is to take the control away from my reason. My mind has been in control all of my life, and it would kill me rather than relinquish control. At one point in my apprenticeship I became profoundly depressed. I was overwhelmed with terror and gloom and thoughts about suicide. Then don Juan warned me this was one of reason's tricks to retain control. He said my reason was making my body feel that there was no meaning to life. Once my mind waged this last battle and lost, reason began to assume its proper place as a tool of the body.

Keen: "The heart has its reasons that reason knows nothing of" and so does the rest of the body.

Castaneda: That is the point. The body has a will of its own. Or rather, the will is the voice of the body. That is why don Juan consistently put his teachings in dramatic form. My intellect could easily dismiss his world of sorcery as nonsense. But my body was attracted to his world and his way of life. And once the body took over, a new and healthier reign was established.

Keen: Don Juan's techniques for dealing with dreams engaged me because they suggest the possibility of voluntary control of dream images. It is as though he proposes to establish a permanent, stable observatory within inner space. Tell me about don Juan's dream training.

Castaneda: The trick in dreaming is to sustain dream images long enough to look at them carefully. To gain this kind of control you need to pick one thing in advance and learn to find it in your dreams. Don Juan suggested that I use my hands as a steady point and go back and forth between them and the images. After some months I learned to find my hands and to stop the dream. I became so fascinated with the technique that I could hardly wait to go to sleep.

Keen: Is stopping the images in dreams anything like stopping the world?

Castaneda: It is similar. But there are differences. Once you are capable of finding your hands at will, you realize that it is only a technique. What you are after is control. A man of knowledge must accumulate personal power. But that is not enough to stop the world. Some abandon also is necessary. You must silence the chatter that is going on inside your mind and surrender yourself to the outside world.

Keen: Of the many techniques that don Juan taught you for stopping the world, which do you still practice?

Castaneda: My major discipline now is to disrupt my routines. I was always a very routinary person. I ate and slept on schedule. In 1965 I began to change my habits. I wrote in the quiet hours of the night and slept and ate when I felt the need. Now I have dismantled so many of my habitual ways of acting that before long I may become unpredictable and surprising to myself.

Keen: Your discipline reminds me of the Zen story of two disciples bragging about miraculous powers. One disciple claimed the founder of the sect to which he belonged could stand on one side of a river and write the name of Buddha on a piece of paper held by his assistant on the opposite shore. The second disciple replied that such a miracle was unimpressive. "My miracle," he said, "is that when I feel hungry

I eat, and when I feel thirsty I drink."

Castaneda: It has been this element of engagement in the world that has kept me following the path which don Juan showed me. There is no need to transcend the world. Everything we need to know is right in front of us if we pay attention. If you enter a state of nonordinary reality, as you do when you use psychotropic plants, it is only to draw from it what you need in order to see the miraculous character of ordinary reality. For me the way to live—the path with heart—is not introspection or mystical transcendence but presence in the world. This world is the warrior's hunting ground.

Keen: The world you and don Juan have pictured is full of magical coyotes, enchanted crows, and a beautiful sorceress. It's easy to see how it could engage you. But what about the world of the modern urban person? Where is the magic there? If we could all live in the mountains we might keep wonder alive. But how is it possible when we are half a zoom from the freeway?

Castaneda: I once asked don Juan the same question. We were sitting in a cafe in Yuma and I suggested that I might be able to learn to stop the world and to see, if I could come and live in the wilderness with him. He looked out the window at the passing cars and said, "That, out there, is your world. You cannot refuse it. You are a hunter of that world." I live in Los Angeles now, and I find I can use that world to accommodate my needs. It is a challenge to live with no set routines in a routinary world. But it can be done.

Keen: The noise level and the constant pressure of masses of people seem to destroy the silence and solitude that would be essential for stopping the world.

Castaneda: Not at all. In fact, the noise can be used. You can use the buzzing of the freeway to teach yourself to listen to the outside world. When we stop the world, the world we stop is the one we usually maintain by our continual inner dialogue. Once you can stop the internal babble you stop maintaining your old world. The descriptions collapse. That is when personality change begins. When you concentrate on sounds, you realize it is difficult for the brain to categorize all the sounds, and in a short while you stop trying. This is unlike visual perception which keeps us forming categories and thinking. It is so restful when you can turn off the talking, categorizing, and judging.

Keen: The internal world changes but what about the external one? We may revolutionize individual consciousness but still not touch the social structures that create our alienation. Is there any place for social or political reform in your thinking?

Castaneda: I came from Latin America, where intellectuals were always talking about political and social revolution and where a lot of bombs were thrown. But revolution hasn't changed much. It takes little daring to bomb a building, but in order to give up cigarettes or to stop being anxious or to stop internal chattering, you have to remake yourself. That is where real reform begins.

Don Juan and I were in Tucson not long ago when they were having Earth Week. Some man was lecturing on ecology and the evils of the war in Vietnam. All the while he was smoking. Don Juan said, "I cannot imagine that he is concerned with other people's bodies when he doesn't like his own." Our first concern should be with ourselves. I can like my fellowmen only when I am at my peak of vigor and am not depressed. To be in this condition I must keep my body trimmed. Any revolution must begin here in this body. I can alter my culture but only from within a body that is impeccably tuned-in to this weird world. For me, the real accomplishment is the art of being a warrior, which, as don Juan says, is the only way to balance the terror of being a man with the wonder of being a man.

"We Have No Desire to Strengthen the Ego or Make It Happy"

A CONVERSATION WITH OSCAR ICHAZO

When the death of God was announced a few years back some believers and some skeptics suspected He might pop back to life before long. Gods survive better than atheists; they disappear in the winter of our disillusionment, change shapes and costumes, and are resurrected in the spring. If the prophets and gurus of the consciousness revolution are to be believed, God has been reborn and we are rapidly approaching the Omega Point, the Great Awakening, the New Age of the Spirit.

Even to the skeptical observer, a new religious sensitivity is obvious in the widespread interest in Transcendental Meditation, yoga, Sufism, Scientology and the occult arts. Scores of roshis, lamas, swamis, 14-year-old perfect masters, middle-aged wise men, and other realized beings are crisscrossing the United States dispensing a new religion to eager audiences. All this may be a fad. Or we may be at the beginning of a religious reformation more radical than anything that has happened in the West since Calvin got married to capitalism and gave birth to the modern industrial state.

Despite considerable differences, the advocates of the new religion agree in their rejection of the limited view of consciousness that has characterized Western culture. The human mind is not a machine enclosed within a series of constricting Chinese boxes —the head, the body, the environment, the historical moment. It is nothing less than a part of the Divine Intelligence that is

129

homogenized into the entire cosmos. Man, the argument goes, is a cosmological rather than a psychological animal. We are spirit within Spirit, consciousness within Consciousness, void within Void, atman within Brahman, god within God. With the resurgence of a cosmic definition of consciousness comes a rejection of the dualisms that have haunted the Judeo-Christian world: God and man, the supernatural and the natural, the sacred and the secular, faith and reason, science (psychology) and religion.

The new religion is challenging the psychological approach to understanding and curing human dis-ease. It is offering both a new anthropology and a new therapeutic, which begin with the assumption that psychology is a manifestation of the disease for which it purports to be the cure.

As a separate science, psychology was born as God was dying in the nineteenth century. Once Christianity had chased the great god Pan from the wild places of nature and the machine drove him from the heavens, man's only hope of saving himself came from within his psyche. The ego was assigned the role of the missing God. And this, according to the new gurus, is the problem. If we begin with the premise that man is an alien in the cosmos, then all we can do is strengthen the walls that keep us within our self-imposed prisons and learn to cope with loneliness. But true therapy consists in ridding ourselves of the illusion of individuality and dissolving our egocentrism in cosmic consciousness.

There is no better place to savor the distilled essence of the new religious consciousness than the Arica Institute. Arica opened its doors in New York in 1971 to 76 people, most of whom had heard of the teachings of its founder, Oscar Ichazo, from a group of Esalen pilgrims who had been at the original school in Arica, Chile. In two years Arica has grown to have a staff of 250 teachers, centers in New York, San Francisco and Los Angeles, and training programs in a dozen other cities. The curriculum of the school is an amalgam of techniques and disciplines taken from esoteric and religious traditions of the East and West that have been streamlined to give modern Americans a practical path toward almost guaranteed enlightenment. At the New York headquarters (24 West 57th Street) an escalator whisks students and visitors up through a draped tunnel to a carpeted suite of rooms that are colorfully decorated with symbols—tarot cards, yin-yang, diagrams of the levels of satori. Here meditation, mantras, mudras, eurythmics, drumming, yoga, and the latest encounter and group techniques are mixed with lectures on philosophy and diet to form a system of thought and practice that raises the consciousness of the group to a state of enlightenment.

Oscar Ichazo talks with assurance about the coming revolution in consciousness and about the hope that Arica can train sufficient teachers to help the new awakening happen fast enough to save Western culture from the death toward which it is otherwise speeding. The facts he chooses to reveal about his life and training are few and misty. His expert knowledge of the maps of human consciousness and ancient and modern techniques for traveling in psychic space is obvious. Although Arica is largely the result of his vision, he is gradually receding into the background as the organization and spiritual technology he has created begin the job of teaching the mysteries of the higher consciousness which is aborning.

Sam Keen: In the Arica Institute you seem to have created the nearest thing we now have to a university for altered states of consciousness. In your curriculum I can spot ego-reducing and consciousness-raising techniques borrowed from Zen, Sufism, Buddhism, psychoanalysis, encounter, the Gurdjieff work, and many others. How did you come to be a master and teacher of such a large variety of different techniques from so many different religious and esoteric traditions?

Oscar Ichazo: That's a long story. Arica is not as much my invention as it is a product of our times. The knowledge I have contributed to the school came to me from many sources I encountered in my peculiar quest. You might say that I began my exploration of consciousness not to reach altered states of awareness but to escape from them. But that story begins very early in childhood.

Keen: Then let's begin there.

Ichazo: I was raised in Bolivia and Peru. My parents were formally Roman Catholic but had no deep religious interest. I went to a Jesuit school and learned about the theology of the church. Then, quite suddenly, I began to have attacks which came at those moments when I was between waking and sleeping. The first time it happened (on December 20, 1937) I was six and a half years old. The attacks were very violent, not epileptic, but like that. First, I would experience a lot of pain and the fear that I was going to die, and my heart would pound. Then it would stop, the pain would increase and I would die. After a while I would return to my body and discover that I was alive. These attacks began to happen every two or three days. I was terrified but I knew my parents couldn't help me so I didn't say anything to them. I became very lonely and felt different from everyone else. I was constantly afraid that the next attack would be the last or that my parents might think I was dead when I was only out of my body, so I worried obsessively about how I might return to normality.

Keen: Were the images and visions you saw when you were out of your body pleasurable or painful?

Ichazo: Both. When you are in your astral body, both fear and ecstasy can be multiplied to infinite proportions because there are no limits within pure consciousness. It was this that led to my first disillusionment with the church. When the priest taught about hell, I would say to myself, "Last night I was in hell and it wasn't like that." And the paradise of the church didn't come any closer to the one I saw in my travels. Still, I thought communion and prayer might help me get rid of my fearful obsession, but they only made it worse. I was like a man who took LSD with the hope that something miraculous would happen and . . . nothing. Prayer only made me focus more firmly on my problem.

Keen: How did you begin to circle out of your obsession?

Ichazo: I made the discovery that being caught in my own subjectivity was hell and there were things I could do to get me out of hell.

Keen: After the standard means of grace failed you took responsibility for the control of your own consciousness.

Ichazo: A little bit. At least the idea was there, but it took me many years to gain the control. I started reading everything I could find on anatomy, physiology, and medicine with the hope of finding out what to do about my condition. Then I had the good fortune to be introduced to the martial arts. I started samurai training and had my first introduction to Zen meditation. My family owned some land so I had contact with the Indians, and they introduced me to psychedelic drugs and shamanism while I was in my early teens. I also began to experiment with hypnotism and to practice yoga. And all the while I was reading all the philosophy I could get ahold of—especially William James. At seventeen I went to the University at La Paz, but I was bored and disappointed and very much alone.

Keen: The tension is building, so we must be getting near the punch line.

Ichazo: When I was nineteen, a remarkable man found me in La Paz. He was sixty years old, and when he began to teach me, I knew from the beginning that he was speaking the truth. This man, whose name I have pledged not to reveal, belonged to a small group in Buenos Aires that met to share their knowledge of various esoteric consciousness-altering techniques. I became the coffee boy for this group. I would get up at 4:00 A.M. to make their coffee and breakfast and would stay around as inconspicuously as possible. Gradually they got used to my presence, and they started using me as a guinea pig to demonstrate techniques to each other. To settle arguments about whether some particular kind of meditation or mantra worked, they would have me try it and report what I experienced.

Keen: What kinds of disciplines were being shared in the group?

Ichazo: About two-thirds of the group were Orientals, so they were strong on Zen, Sufism, and Cabala. They also used some techniques I later found in the Gurdjieff work.

Keen: Where does the story go from here?

Ichazo: One day when I was serving coffee, an argument arose between two members of the group. I turned to one and said, "You are not right. He is right." Just like that. Then I explained the point until both of them understood. This incident changed everything. They asked me to leave and I thought I was being kicked out for being pretentious. But after about a week, they called me back and told me they had all decided to teach me. They worked with me for two more years and then opened doors for me in the Orient. After a time of remaining at home in Chile, I began to travel and study in the East, in Hong Kong, India, and Tibet. I did more work in the martial arts, learned all of the higher yogas, studied Buddhism and Confucianism, alchemy and the wisdom of the *I Ching*. Then I went back to La Paz to live with my father and digest my learnings. After working alone for a year, I went into a divine coma for seven days. When I came out of it, I knew that I should teach; it was impossible that all my good luck should be only for myself. But it took me two years to act on this decision. Then I went to Santiago and started lecturing in the Institute for Applied Psychology. Things got so busy and crowded there that I decided to move to the remote little town of Arica and filter out all except the really committed persons who would follow me there. At first I worked with a group of ten. Then in 1970, a group of Americans —about fifty—came and stayed for nine months. Fifteen of these were from Esalen. It was clear to me that the time had come to move the work to North America. So here we are—The Arica Institute with centers in New York, Los Angeles and San Francisco.

Keen: Every form of therapy, whether it is carried on in churches, growth centers, consulting rooms, or wisdom school, rests upon a vision of what man might become, a diagnosis of his present unhappiness and a prescription for how he may move toward fulfillment. What kind of an animal is a human being?

Ichazo: We have to distinguish between man as he is in essence and as he is in ego or personality. In essence every person is perfect, fearless, and in a loving unity with the entire cosmos; there is no conflict within the person between head, heart, and stomach or between the person and others. Every human being starts in pure essence. Then something happens: the ego begins to develop; karma accumulates; there is a transition from objectivity to subjectivity; man falls from essence into personality.

Keen: Is the fall an historical incident? Or are you talking about some mythical event like the expulsion from the Garden of Eden, or the class conflict that developed when the bourgeois began to exploit the proletariat, or the childhood replay of the drama of Oedipus or Electra?

Ichazo: A person retains the purity of essence for a short time. It is lost between four and six years of age when the child begins to imitate his parents, tell lies, and pretend. A contradiction develops between the inner feelings of the child and the outer social reality to which he must conform. Ego consciousness is the limited mode of awareness that develops as a result of the fall into society. Personality forms a defensive layer over the essence, and so there is a split between the self and the world. The ego feels the world as alien and dangerous because it constantly fails to satisfy the deeper needs of the self.

Keen: Erik Erikson describes the same process as the failure to maintain a relationship of basic trust. Society is based upon that mild form of schizophrenia we call "normality."

Ichazo: Another way to characterize the ego is as the principle of compensation for an imagined loss. When we turn away from our primal perfection, our completeness, our unity with the world and God, we create the illusion that we need something exterior to ourselves for our completion. This dependency on what is exterior is what makes man's ego. Once man is within ego consciousness, he is driven by desire and fear. He can find no real happiness until desire is extinguished and he returns to his essence, that is, until he reaches what Buddhism called nirvana or the Void.

Keen: The question of desire seems to be the crucial point that separates Eastern and Western visions of man. Buddhism and Eastern religion in general see desire as something that must be purged before man can be happy, but Western philosophers and psychologists tend to believe that if we can separate our conscious and unconscious desires we can strengthen the ego to deal with reality and achieve happiness. I think Plato's myth of the birth of erotic love is archetypical for the Western mind. Originally human beings were joined back to back in pairs. Pairs came in three varieties, male-male, female-female, male-female. The gods took compassion on them and split them apart so they could face each other and make love. Erotic love is the drive to be reunited with our lost half. We desire because we are incomplete. The deepest root of desire is the natural dependency between the sexes. Isn't desire rooted in biological differences, in the ontological fact of the incompleteness? Why not accept the need for interdependence rather than try to purge the ego and root out desire for what delights and completes us? Aren't you trying to make the self independent of the world?

Ichazo: No. Only of a certain artificially constructed social world. The illusory world that Buddhism spoke of as maya—illusion—is a socially created idea of what the world is. It is one way of seeing things. So long as we remain within the ego we see the world only through the screen of our fears, our vanity, and our desire.

Keen: And if we shatter the illusions of the ego we can, as don Juan said, "stop the world" and discover reality. If the ego is the devil in man it would be good to understand what it is made up of and how it works. What is this ego you are trying to remove from modern man?

Ichazo: Since ego is false or distorted consciousness, the best way to define it is to back up a step and look more closely at man's essential nature. There are three centers in the human animal: the intellectual, the emotional, and the vital, or as we call them, the path, the oth and the kath. Ideally the kath is the master of life; it is the center which directs vital movement and allows us to relate to the world with instinctual immediacy. We sense our basic unity with all life in our guts.

This idea is common to many wisdom traditions. In the Orient the martial arts concentrated on developing awareness of this center which they located about four inches below the navel. They called it the tantien or the hara.

Keen: And the oth center would be the one traditionally connected with the heart?

Ichazo: Yes. And reason with the path. In short, what happens when ego develops is that the head takes over and tries to direct everything. The ego is made up of words and ideas, endless interior chatter, and repetitious thought patterns that form fixed ways of defending the person against the natural flow of life. Ego creates a whole subjective world that must be defended against objective reality, so it always exists in fear.

Keen: The fundamental human problem, then, is the existence of ego. What is the prescription that will lead us back to health and essence?

Ichazo: Ego is made up of three interconnected parts: it has an intellectual segment, an emotional segment, and a movement segment. Ego reduction involves working with each of these elements. The way we do this in Arica is rather intricate. Do you want the whole theory and practice of ego reduction?

Keen: Well, the best Freud could promise was interminable analysis to strengthen the ego so we could cope with the everlasting discontent of the real world, and most other Western therapeutics promise only improvement or adjustment. So, if you are suggesting that we might be cured of ego altogether, I am interested in hearing the details.

Ichazo: Let's begin with the intellectual aspect of the ego. The difficulty is both that we are always trying to control life with our heads and that so long as we remain in ego we have the wrong ideas about man and his place in the cosmos. Very early in our training we introduce a system of mentations that trains people to think with their entire bodies rather than only with their "minds."

It is a mistake to consider thought the result of one specialized organ, the brain. If there are no internal blocks set up by the ego, each thought is as much a product of the eye or the foot as of the brain-computer. When we are unified, thought and action are the same. We divide the body into twelve parts, each of which has a physiological and a parallel psychological function:

Ears perceive the meaning or *logos* and give us the substance of things.

Eyes isolate forms.

The nose smells out possibilities.

The mouth and the stomach sense our needs for nourishment.

The heart energizes the organism with its impulse.

The liver assimilates food and percepts we take into the organism.

The colon, anus, bladder and kidneys eliminate foods, ideas, and experiences that are unmetabolizable.

The genitals reflect our orientation toward or away from life.

The thighs and upper arms reflect our capacity, or strength.

The knees and elbows reflect the ease or awkwardness, the charisma, with which we move through the world.

The calves and forearms are the means we use.

The hands and feet are used for going and taking, for reaching out for goals.

Keen: How does this technique work? If, for instance, I were considering whether I should get a serious job or take off for Tahiti, would I begin with my goals and think the problem through with all of the other parts of my body?

Ichazo: That is one way the mentations are used. Any question or problem you are considering can be thought through more completely by allowing each part of the body to become infused with consciousness. There are also times when you become specially aware of some part of the body. If, for instance, you are having trouble with your kidneys you need to ask what things in your life must be eliminated. More generally the mentations are used to condition the entire body to tune itself to the world. Once consciousness is homogenized into the entire organism, the head is emptied and it ceases to exert a tyrannical control over everything.

Keen: The idea of overthrowing the domination of the head and spreading consciousness more democratically in other parts of the body—participatory democracy in the body and the body politic—

seems to be emerging in many different places these days. Norman O. Brown wants to see us have "polymorphously perverse" bodies, don Juan's "man of knowledge" has fibers of light that connect his solar plexus to the world, and the advocates of Zen are inviting us to practice "no mind." A lot of people in Western culture are tired of mind tripping and look to the body as the new Eden. But if we have to lose our heads to find our tails we are only flipping the coin. I sometimes think we are in danger of forgetting what Plato and Aristotle taught us—the mind is an erogenous zone. We need to use it more to caress and care for the world and less to manipulate it.

Ichazo: I would agree. We are not anti-intellectual. The techniques we use are designed only to destroy ego-dominated thought. We believe there are ideas a person must understand in order to be whole. Not only must we change the way we think, but we must change what we think. We call the intellectual part of the ego the fixation, and each fixation is remedied by an idea. Every person develops a style of compensating for the lack, the ontological emptiness, which is at the center of the ego. We say there are nine basic styles or points of ego fixation. The easiest way for me to explain the fixations and the ideas that cure them is to use the diagrams (enneagrams) we have developed. (See p. 140.)

Let's take one ego-type and see how this schema works. The indolent type of person may be very energetic in his relations with the outside world, but he does not take responsibility for cultivating his essence. This fixation roots in an especially keen awareness of the absence of love and therefore of a sense of lacking being. The indolent type goes out looking for the love and meaning he feels deprived of; he becomes a continual seeker, but never a finder. This is his trap. He is always searching outside of himself for what can only be found within. But in a perverse way the seeker is ignorant about himself. He believes he knows all about other people and he doesn't hesitate to tell everyone else. The hell of the indolent is the worst of all the fixations because it leads to inner paralysis and indecision. The ego-indolent is always working very hard seeking but until the last moment before

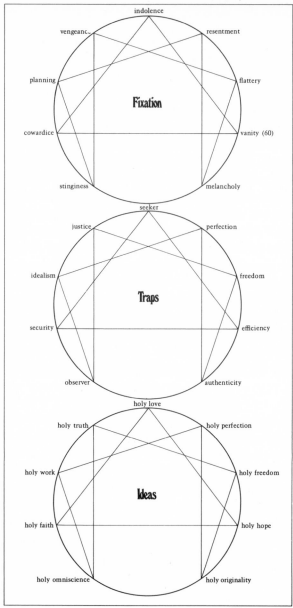

Fixation

indolence
vengeanc~
resentment
planning
flattery
cowardice
vanity (60)
stinginess
melancholy

Traps

seeker
justice
perfection
idealism
freedom
security
efficiency
observer
authenticity

Ideas

holy love
holy truth
holy perfection
holy work
holy freedom
holy faith
holy hope
holy omniscience
holy originality

the fixation breaks he vacillates and never quite takes the responsibility for his own life. He is always dealing with the largest issues of identity and destiny—total truth and total perfection—but he feels how far he is from being able to love and act authentically. The indolent person frequently tries to use sex to gain love. He makes the whole world over into the image of the absent mother. *The Confessions of St. Augustine* is a good illustration of the inner world of the indolent type. Augustine remained a seeker until he allowed God to find him.

Keen: The more you talk about the inner dynamics of this fixation the more it sounds like a description of the universal human condition. There is a void at the center of every psyche. You can call it the absent mother, nothingness, ontological anxiety, divine restlessness, or the unreasonable fear of death. But it seems to be characteristic of every person.

Ichazo: It is a fundamental condition of all ego consciousness but some people are more aware of it than others. The indolent fixation is at the head of the enneagram because it focuses on the most universal aspect of the ego's deprivation. In the same way the remedy for indolence is in some way the remedy which cures all egos—the idea of holy love.

Love starts in the moment a man contemplates the creation and says "Thank You, God." The Holy Spirit really takes care of the universe; it is the active principle of love in all things. And it is only by getting in touch with this spirit that the indolence of the ego is transformed into active love. Holy love breaks the indolence and removes the feeling of separateness. With holy love comes the awareness that although the laws which govern reality are objective, they are not cold, because they lead to the creation of organic life that fulfills a cosmic purpose.

Keen: I would like to go on a small tangent. Your theory of personality goes back to the traditional religious affirmation that man has no secure identity apart from the knowledge of his divine origin and destiny. Lacking knowledge of what Thomas Aquinas called the perfections of God, man tries to compensate. The various ego fixations are merely varieties of ignorance of the divine. Is psychic health possible apart from a religious view of the world? Can't we save the ego rather than get rid of it?

Ichazo: We have no desire to strengthen the ego or to make it happy. Short of enlightenment there is no way to harmonize and unify the psyche. When man is in essence he knows he is within the divine unity. Only then does the dreadful alienation of the ego with all of its defensiveness and fear disappear. There is no peace short of being within the divine consciousness. It should be clear by now that the Western secular attempt to live without knowledge of the sacred unity of all things is a failure.

Keen: Are you proposing a new religion? And is Arica a new church?

Ichazo: Not at all. The disciplines we teach are very old. Many of them are adapted from traditional Buddhist, Taoist, Islamic, or Christian sources. But we do not have any creed or dogma. We introduce people to techniques that facilitate experiences, but we are experimental in our approach. We do not ask for any belief or faith. We only say: try these things and see what happens to you. But the group, the community, is an important part of the work. When people see others with their same ego fixation they feel less alone and less serious about their hang-ups. We do the work of ego reduction with a lot of humor and laughter. And all this helps. When a person feels a part of a community of fools or sinners, he begins to realize that the pretensions of the ego are no longer necessary.

Keen: It appears that you are grafting an Eastern understanding of the human condition onto a Western society. I wonder both how effective and salutary it will be. Western religion and psychology made an effort to free man from consciousness, from excessive introspection. Both Christianity and Freud defined maturity in terms of the ability to love and to work. Your trip seems to increase introspection to the point where it becomes a total preoccupation. Meditations, mantras, and mudras seem to fill the day of the Arica student.

Ichazo: Any form of meditation or discipline to raise consciousness initially creates greater self-consciousness because the ego reacts with fear to the threat that it may die. But as the essence is nourished by the disciplines and the love within the group, ego consciousness is lost, and there is a new awareness and appreciation of the world. Our aim is not to detach people from this world but to train them to change it—to slow down and love the earth—before it is too late.

Keen: Let's get back to some of the other techniques for destroying the ego. How do you deal with the emotional component of the ego?

Ichazo: There are certain biological understandings within the body which naturally result in a harmonious emotional life. These are the objective virtues. An essential individual will be in contact with these constantly, simply by living in his body. But the subjective individual, the ego, loses touch with these virtues. Then the personality attempts to compensate by developing passions. The passions which are a product of the mind alone can be seen as the subjective expression of the lack of the objective virtues. Again the fastest and clearest way to see the relation of these ideas is to use the enneagrams. (See p. 145.)

Let's follow the example that we began earlier. The top place on the enneagram is the dominant passion for the indolent ego type: laziness. Laziness refers to avoidance of the work required to develop essence, and it is a compensation for the lack of the virtue action. True activity takes place when the body is healthy and receptive to energy from the kath. This can happen only when the head is empty, that is, in satori. Activity doesn't result from a command of the mind . . . You can go on around the points of enneagram and do a comparable analysis for the other ego types.

We have many techniques for dealing with the emotional component of ego structure and we are always experimenting with new methods. Since fear is a defense mechanism of the ego connected with protecting an image of the self, we sometimes have people compile a long list of words that are insulting to them. Then we work with these until they have been emotionally neutralized. We also make use of mudras—body positions like the āsanas in yoga—that create a disposition for the objective virtues. These are stances and gestures that give the feeling of courage or humility. An important part of our work is creating a sensitivity to different ways of breathing; shallow upper-chest breathing is typical of ego consciousness, while kath breathing is more characteristic of the person who is in essence. We teach the art of creating rituals and ceremonies, liturgies for the new spiritual consciousness. And, of course, since many of our teachers are ex-Esalenists, we use many of the techniques of self-knowledge that have been developed in humanistic psychology.

Keen: You have saved the best for last. How do we reach the state of blessedness when the mind is empty of chatter, defenses, plans, and games, and the kath is the master of life?

Ichazo: That is a little bit like asking, "What are your techniques for doing nothing?" When we are in perfect awareness we know nothing and we are immediately in the action of nonaction. It happens naturally. In China they called this *wu wei.* In Taoism nature moves you, you don't move it. All of our work is aimed toward this goal, but nothing we do makes it happen. When the ego is broken the essence quite naturally takes over. The collapse comes at the moment when the ego games are completely exposed and understood, illusion is shattered; subjectivity is destroyed; karma is burned.

Keen: Perhaps the moment of grace cannot be programed, but you do have a whole technology for developing awareness of the kath.

Ichazo: Yes. The transfer of consciousness from head to kath is a constant emphasis of the Arica program but the work with movement, breathing, and mantra focuses especially on this problem. We have a program of regular exercises that tone up the body and make it flexible. We use things like African dance, eurythmics, and drumming to develop kath awareness. The mantras and chants increase body awareness by training people to feel sound and vibrations in the various centers of the body. Probably the strongest and most ancient methods we use are the respiratory techniques.

What Eastern philosophers referred to as prana yoga we call alpha

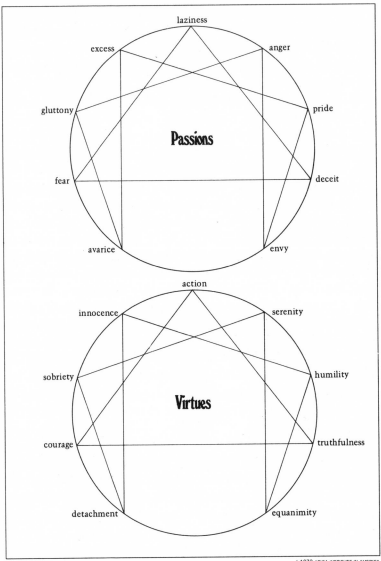

Passions

laziness
excess   anger
gluttony   pride
fear   deceit
avarice   envy

Virtues

action
innocence   serenity
sobriety   humility
courage   truthfulness
detachment   equanimity

"We Have No Desire to Strengthen the Ego"   145

breathing. The same alpha frequencies that are in our brains are also in the ionosphere; so, we can unite the psyche and the cosmos in the act of breathing. In ego breathing the head controls by interrupting the natural flow. In natural breathing we stop ordering the lungs and become receptive to the way the organism wants to breathe. In the moment when we let go we realize that we do not have to make ourselves breathe: He is breathing us.

Keen: The image of breath seems to be central to most religious traditions. Our words "animal" and "spirit" and "inspiration" all go back to the root image of "breathe." In the Hebraic tradition man became man at the point when God breathed His spirit into him. More recently psychology seems to have discovered what yoga practitioners have known for centuries—anxiety is always accompanied by interrupted respiration.

The consciousness revolution we are experiencing is in some way connected with the rediscovery of breathing. When we concentrate on breathing we see the paradox that we keep consciously interfering with a process that works perfectly naturally so long as it remains unconscious. Our split between doing and allowing, between conscious command of the whole of life and surrender to natural rhythms that are not of our making is symbolically dramatized in our breathing. The age of anxiety is the age of over-controlled breath. The new spiritual revolution is animated by the hope of finding our way back to the power that breathes us, to the force that lives beneath the level of our conscious minds.

Ichazo: As a culture, our awareness is beginning to shift from ego to kath. The process of awakening in humanity is parallel to the process in an individual. We are no longer on an individual trip. The whole society is raising its consciousness. All history up to this point has been winter. Now spring is coming for sure. We are living in the time of the transformation.

Keen: What evidence do you have that the "consciousness revolution" is a great awakening and not merely another fad?

Ichazo: The contradictions within Western culture have reached such massive proportions that we either must change or die. We are similar to the man who sees that his ego only produces greater conflict, competition, suspicion and fear. The logic of technology is driving us faster and faster into a culture of perpetual change in which we are exhausting both our psyches and our natural resources. The way of life that creates a hunger in us for more and more, faster and faster, leaves us unsatisfied. The hope for both personal and cultural transformation lies in the fact that ego always ends up killing ego. When the velocity toward satisfying ego needs increases to a certain point the whole ego system collapses; the absurdity and contradictions are suddenly obvious. This is the first satori. Our culture is now experiencing the first moment of enlightenment.

Keen: There is another, less optimistic, way to interpret the consciousness revolution. It may be the sign of the death rather than the rebirth of our culture. The traditional Western dream was that we could know and control nature in sufficient degree to create "an alabaster city undimmed by human tears." But our ethic of work and our obsession with the technological dream have produced Vietnam, trips to the moon, and a hopelessness about fundamental political and social changes. There is no American dream. We seem to have lost our nerve. And so we are turning inward. If we can't change the exterior world we can at least change our consciousness. I sometimes think three million people a month read *Psychology Today* in hope of finding some succor for a lost something they used to call their souls.

Ichazo: That is a possible way of looking at things, but I think it is wrong. Too many forces are converging to make an awakening inevitable. Take the media, for instance; they are the nervous system of the culture. So now the nervous system is getting connected. Television and computers give us fast feedback from the extremities of our social organism to the central nervous system. We are becoming more sensitive. We see and feel what we are doing to ourselves with our insane velocity.

Keen: But vision can be blinding. It may be, as Zorba said, that we are too damn sensitive. We may have immobilized ourselves with sensitivity. And the sign of this immobilization may be that the people, who a couple of years ago were outraged enough to want to change the culture, are now moving into the inner world. Jerry Rubin is reputed to have given up the politics of confrontation for bioenergetics. Many of my friends who were in the Radical Left are now more involved in body therapies—Rolfing, sensitivity, Reichian therapy—than in the body politic.

Ichazo: But even the paralysis may be a sign of the end of the old order. In the ego-indolent fixation, for instance, right before the ego breaks there is tremendous exterior movement combined with interior paralysis. And also the cultural elite are already beyond the materialistic dream and are rediscovering the spiritual unity of the cosmos.

From a practical perspective we need a cosmic vision to create the ecological consciousness necessary to survive on this planet. The world is not limitless, so we must discover that humanity is one body. If the idea of reincarnation is real—and it is—then all the people who ever existed in the world are now alive. We all are now. Humanity is the Messiah and we are awakening to that fact. That is the meaning of the consciousness revolution.

Keen: Maybe. Maybe. I wish I had your confidence. But I look at history and see too many times when we have been at similar points and there have been similar apocalyptic philosophies. Someone has always been proclaiming the end of the world, and the world to their embarrassment kept on its muddled, ambivalent way. Jesus and the Essenes read the signs of the times and saw the Kingdom of God approaching. So did Kant and Hegel and the thinkers of the Enlightenment. Visions of Utopia, enlightenment, and the best of all possible worlds are dangerous because they make us discontent with the actual world and make coping seem like a compromise. When Kierkegaard said to Hegel, "I am only a limited existing human being. I cannot stand outside of my historical condition in order to see the unfolding of the Absolute Spirit," he was giving the existentialist warning against the visions of an idealist. Or, as a Buddhist tradition says: samsara is nirvana. This world of suffering is where we find happiness;

it isn't the best of all possible worlds, it is only the best one we have. And the danger is that visions of the awakening of God become so easily politicized. Hegel saw the German state as the incarnation of the Absolute Spirit in history and we see the American state as the defensive arm of the God in whom we trust to make the world safe for democracy. Whenever you have a utopian vision there is always a Grand Inquisitor hidden in back of the scenes pulling the strings to make things happen in the right and holy manner.

Ichazo: In past eras the mystical trip was an individual matter, or at least a matter of small groups, but no longer. This is what is new in human history. Everybody can now achieve a higher degree of consciousness. We can all take this trip together. True democracy is based on the fact that in essence we are all equal and perfect. So the idea of a leader for the new consciousness revolution is no longer necessary. It is more that humanity is an organic body that goes through the same stages an individual does on the path toward enlightenment. In Western culture competition has reached such a velocity that consciousness must inevitably change. When the ego or a society reaps the full hell they have sown in their quest for false security and status, they come to the point of collapse and rebirth. Already the new vision of the world is capturing the young people. Our minds are enlarging and our aims becoming more universal. The vision of humanity as one enormous family, one objective tribe, may once have been utopian. Now it is a practical necessity.

"We Do Not *Have* Bodies, We *Are* Our Bodies"

A CONVERSATION WITH STANLEY KELEMAN

After the failure of many a revolution, we are returning home to our bodies. Black is beautiful, gay is good, and no male legislator has the right to tell a woman how, when, or where to grow a baby. And no body (politic) can send this body off to kill other bodies (men, women, and children) who have been defined as enemies. Even the WASPs are beginning to smell flowers, practice sensitivity, and suspect that it might not profit a man much to gain the world if he loses the capacity to enjoy it. No telling where it all ends. Someday we may be liberated from beauty and ugly, 36-24-36, and the tyranny that makes destiny out of the fortunate placement of a few inches of fat tissue or the size of a nose.

Stanley Keleman is a celebrant of biological life. If we had Earthfathers, he might be one. He looks like and moves with the authority of a large and probably friendly bear. The massive iron sculptures of hovering birds he welds in his spare time suggest his rare combination of power and tenderness. It is not hard to believe the rumors of the California grapevine that he is one of the most effective therapists in the bioenergetic movement, or to understand why there are long waiting lists for the workshops he gives at growth centers across the country. Keleman's recent writings (*Bioenergetic Concepts of Grounding; Todtmoos; Sexuality, Self and Survival,* Lodestar Press, P.O. Box 31003, San Francisco, California 94131) evidence a growing ability to create a

153

new theory of embodiment which improves on the early efforts of Wilhelm Reich.

Keleman's authority is largely homegrown. He created a therapeutic style from diverse elements he found in his quest for a way to live the wisdom of the body. The son of immigrants from Hungary and Romania, he grew up in Brooklyn. He had difficulty in school because, as he says, "I knew a lot of answers but couldn't tell how I got them." His athletic ability won him scholarships to several colleges and he spent some time at two or three of them; that was enough to convince him that the answers he wanted were not to be found in the academy. The question that haunted him was, what does it mean to experience my self? His suspicion that self-knowledge must begin in the body led him to the out-of-the-way institutions and people who were then experimenting with ways to put the body at the center of the therapeutic enterprise. His teachers were all outlaws who denied the orthodox wisdom of the day; problems of the mind were to be dealt with by psychiatrists and problems of the body by physicians, and never the twain would meet, except in the pineal gland or in professional associations dealing with psychosomatic medicine.

At the Chiropractic Institute of New York he learned that postural distortion was specifically related to disease and that the body could be reorganized. At the Bioenergetic Institute, under Alexander Lowen, he came into contact with the theory and practice of Reichian therapy. During the same period he studied privately with Nina Bull, the developer of attitude psychology, and attended seminars at the Alfred Adler Institute. In 1963 he went to Europe where he worked with Karlfried Durckheim, one of the original Gestalt researchers, and with Dori Gutscher of Dasein Analytic Institute. Then, in 1966, home to California to spend eight months in residence at Esalen. He now lives and practices in Berkeley, where revolution is always at least discussed. His Center for Energetic Studies at 1645 Virginia Street is the home base; he does his writing there. He currently has two books, one on death and one on the formative process, in the typewriter. His emphasis on the body and the importance of grounding mirrors a new awareness that is likely to be a part of the politics of the future. The radical demands now are for conservation, for a return to the roots. We all want to get back to the place we never left—embodiment in the living earth.

Sam Keen: When I made my first pilgrimage to the notorious growth centers of California in 1968, it was the sights and sounds of a workshop in bioenergetics conducted by Stanley Keleman at Kairos that most shocked my modesty. The nudity at the Esalen baths seemed rather sedate; flute music and incense combined with the rhythmic surge of the Pacific to create a sense of calm and order. But you were encouraging people to hit, kick, scream, and to yield to the involuntary pulsations of their bodies. You were teaching them how to lose control. I knew you were a libertine and very probably an agent of the forces of chaos and irrationality. Since that time I have come to appreciate bioenergetics as one of the major therapeutic paths to the sanity and wisdom of the body.

What are the defining characteristics of bioenergetics as you practice it?

Stanley Keleman: Bioenergetics focuses on the movement and form of the human organism. It tries to understand the relationship between emotion and motion, structure and process. We say that a person is a life process, a moving structure, a body in motion. And all emotional or psychological conflicts involve a distortion of body movement. To free the self is to free the body.

Keen: How does your practice differ from that of a Freudian, Jungian, or a Primal therapist?

Keleman: My first interest is in a person's body presence. I look to see how much coordination and grace there is in the body, where it is weak or rigid, what parts are overdeveloped or have too little development, how much vitality is obvious. And I try to locate the physical and psychic constrictions that have become habitual.

Keen: Is there a universal language of the body? Do bodily stances correlate with emotional dispositions?

Keleman: My reading of the language of the body is based on working assumptions. Stiffness in the neck or spine or locked legs generally indicate fear of instability and the necessity to inhabit life with firmness. Where the muscles are weak or tend to collapse it is an indication that the person cannot stand a lot of excitation or conflict. There are recognizable patterns: hysterical bodies are overactive, self-defeating; masochistic bodies are dense and heavily muscled; schizoid bodies are fragmented, the parts don't seem to go together, some are overstiff and others weak.

Keen: The poker and the marshmallow or the hypertonic and the atonic represent the extremes in body types.

Keleman: Right. I also divide the body arbitrarily into upper and lower halves. The lower half of the body gives me clues about how a person relates to the instinctual world. Sexuality and excretion reflect the relation to the private instinctual world, and the legs and feet show how a person feels about independence and grounding. The upper body represents the way a person lives in a social world. By noticing the arms, hands, chest, and face I get an idea of how a person reaches out to manipulate and love the world. I am interested in the relation between the instinctual and the social worlds. Is the upper body more developed than the lower? If so, the person may have had a very restrictive upbringing and may have compensated by controlling upper-body movements at the cost of cutting off involuntary sexual feelings and movements. Or the lower half of the body may be overdeveloped. Women who received a lot of reinforcement for being attractive and sexy, for loving their daddies, often are alive and have a lot of movement in their lower bodies but have sunken chests and dull eyes; they look frightened and submissive and lacking in the force necessary to challenge life.

A person's structural and movement patterns are existential statements about how he lives in the world.

Keen: Bioenergetics seems to be the appropriate therapeutic tool for an existentialist theory of man. Gabriel Marcel, Jean-Paul Sartre,

Martin Heidegger insisted that mind is not separable from body. Traditional psychotherapy has an idealistic prejudice; it acknowledges the relationship of psyche and soma, but it tries to instigate the healing process by dealing with ideas, images, words, and memories. The classical "talking cure" of traditional therapy locates the impediments to psychic health more in the mind than the body.

Keleman: I agree completely. We do not *have* bodies, we *are* our bodies. Nor is there a separation between body and world. As embodied beings we manifest our history and demonstrate our interaction with our world. The living body experiences itself and the world in the same way, as closed or open, warm or cold, threatening or promising. Our uniqueness is in this double awareness; we are the world and ourselves, we are our past and our present.

Keen: I am not sure you can solve the mind/body problem so neatly. Don't you just jump on the opposite end of the seesaw, the materialistic rather than the idealistic end? I would hope I do not have to lose my mind to find my body.

Keleman: I don't think bioenergetics is reductionistic. It isn't trying to affirm the body at the cost of the mind. It is proposing an energetic theory of reality which unites body and mind. A short trip into history might clarify this.

Freud dealt largely in the coin of the mind. He worked with fantasies, words, dreams, and memories in an effort to show how the mind works, how it distorts reality and is conditioned by life experience.

Wilhelm Reich attempted to understand man as a biological process and he investigated the common energetic factor behind mind and body. Bioenergetics is an outgrowth of his vision of the single unitary process of which mind and body are different manifestations.

As a therapist I don't think in terms of mind and body. I don't specialize in ideas *or* feelings. I try to see the way a person expresses himself as a holistic statement about his way of being in the world. For instance, when I ask somebody to lie down and kick the bed twenty-five times, I find that the increased breathing and movement triggers sensations, memories, and new perceptions. People will tell me after such an exercise, "I feel tingling in my legs and I remember when I couldn't stand up in the drib and I began to scream and ask for help, but now I feel more like I can stand on my own two feet."

Keen: Is bioenergetics a creation of Wilhelm Reich?

Keleman: He was the granddaddy of us all. He took Freud's idea of libido and made it concrete in physiological and political terms. He developed a theory of character armor which said that distortions of the libido were always manifest in chronic muscular contractions and frozen body dispositions. He saw that major character and body traits had the function of regulating feeling and energy. The physiological and the psychological are two foci of the same process: the character armor shows in the chronic muscular contractions that make a stiff neck, a determined jaw, an overinflated chest, or a tight, flat abdomen. Chronic muscular contractions diminish sensations, diminish movement, and diminish the ability of self-expression and so they encapsulate a limited and unrealistic self-image. If a person cuts off feelings of anger or sexual sensations he will create a self-image that protects his chosen limitations; he will defend a philosophy of life that states that anger is bad and sexuality is a dangerous force needing severe restraints.

Keen: What innovations in therapeutic practice did Reich make to break up the character armor?

Keleman: He would have patients lie on their backs and breathe and feel where the contractions were in their bodies. Then he would ask them to correlate their psychological attitudes and their bodily tensions. He taught them to hit and kick and move, to reach out with the mouth and literally to vomit up psychic poisons they had incorporated. Reich's therapeutic goal was to soften the body sufficiently to allow it to surrender to involuntary pulsations. He saw sexual freedom, the ability of the organism to allow itself to enter into orgasmic states, as the way to recapture independence. And so he concentrated on freeing the pelvis to move in an involuntary way and on freeing the body to yield to its own vibrancy.

Keen: Reich is often accused of overemphasizing sexuality, of preaching a simplistic gospel that more and better orgasms would solve the problems of the world. How much truth is there to this charge?

Keleman: Reich was extremely modest and even Victorian in his sexual expressions. He stressed that the therapeutic goal of orgasmic freedom could not be reached unless a person formed a lasting and meaningful relationship and developed satisfying work. He also was far from naive about the possibility of curing neurosis without major political and social reorganization.

Keen: Reich's reputation is clouded by the grandiosity of his cosmological theories about orgone energy and the strange affair of the orgone accumulators, which the FDA condemned as fraudulent. It seems that the mantle of bioenergetics in this country passed to Alexander Lowen. How has he changed the theory and practice of bioenergetics?

Keleman: In the first place he avoided metaphysics. Where Reich talked mostly about pleasure and the involuntary responses of the organism and stressed softening of the character armor, Lowen has emphasized assertiveness and the ego—the reality principle. Lowen often gets his patients up on their feet to get their energy moving toward the ground. Then he has them hit the bed from this position to get them to mobilize their aggression against their own character blocks. He also holds up the goal of better sexual relationships, but he stresses that a strong ego is necessary in order to surrender to pleasure.

Keen: When any philosophy or therapy emphasizes the pleasure principle, the reality principle is in danger. Norman O. Brown never told us how a person who lived a life of polymorphous perversity could construct an ego with a sense of reality strong enough to plant corn or fix computers. Nor has Herbert Marcuse told us how the garbage would be collected in a society governed by Eros. How do you think about ego, pleasure, and the reality principle?

Keleman: I don't even use the term ego. I replace it with the idea of the social self. The social self is the reality principle. Reality is what

"We Do Not *Have* Bodies, We *Are* Our Bodies"   159

we are willing to support and invest our energy in; it is the range of activities and possibilities to which we commit ourselves. There is no such thing as an objective reality, either cosmological or social, that is separate from our willingness to support it. If the majority of a society suddenly said that the work ethic was all wrong and opted to create a world in which every person could seek his optimum pleasure, that would be the new reality principle. The goals and functions which we support as living organisms define ourselves. We now define ourselves by many functions: reproduction, sexuality, work in relation to survival and in relationship to an ideal. Pleasure is not the only socially desirable reality. Most recently, human beings have invested heavily in analytical and cognitive functions. We describe man as a reasoning animal—*Homo sapiens*—and all other functions have been considered of lesser dignity and value. With Freud's definition of sexuality as the essential factor in human identity, we entered into a new era. I disagree with Freud. I think evolutionary theory points to the fact that man is a becoming. We don't yet know who we are. Or rather, we are biological, energetic processes moving toward an unknown end.

Keen: That brings us back to the question of the relation of the ego and politics. If reality is socially defined, then the structure of the individual is determined by the economic, political, and ideological structures of his time. And if we want to change the person we must change the society. Man has no inside that is unrelated to the outside, no psyche that is uncolored by the polis. It seems to me Reich's genius in creating the foundations for radical therapy has been ignored in the development of bioenergetics in America.

Keleman: I think Lowen was apolitical for good reason. He saw that politics had destroyed Reich. So he assumed the conservative political stance of Freud. Freud knew that if he became a revolutionary too early the whole psychoanalytical movement would be destroyed. In a society dominated by the work ethic, the specter of a life of pleasure is terribly threatening.

Keen: But to try to do body therapy using Freudian concepts of the ego and the reality principle is not merely to lose a single fight, but to surrender in the face of the battle.

If I may translate liberally: the pleasure principle states that pleasure comes before principle; or, in the beginning is love, and then reason *(logos);* or, energy is eternal delight. Or, as Augustine said, "Love and do what you want."

I don't think you can do good therapy without a political (and probably a metaphysical) vision.

Keleman: I agree. For me the idea of evolution is the context of my work. The body is a part of an ongoing process. I don't believe our development of civilization has crippled us. We had to go through the Industrial Revolution and through a period when we overdeveloped our cognitive and manipulatory powers. Certainly, the civilizing process left us with scars; our bodies are armored and deadened to pleasure to some degree. But I don't believe man's cognitive controlling functions are stronger than the life functions. We are unfolding and developing. Everything is in process. Man has gone from being heavily armored to being less armored. Look at the muscle structure of monkeys and apes. And Cro-Magnon man was no candidate for a sensitivity group. Man seems to be getting more erect, thinner-skinned, and more flexible. Our development of year-round sexuality has given us the ability for innovation, and that means an unknown potential. Because we can invent and the pain of the unknown is so great, we have ritualized and structured much of our life. But that is only a temporary process. We now have a far wider range of possible feelings and conduct than our remote ancestors did. So I say it is time to move to a more flexible view of man and to see the earth in transition.

Keen: Freud, Reich, Marcuse, and Brown are all dominated by a romantic vision that decries civilization as a source of discontent and repression. They all long for a return to the noble savage, the unrepressed body of the primitive.

Keleman: All of them seem to have a strange notion of original sin in which the evil is not due to the snake in the garden but the machine

"We Do Not *Have* Bodies, We *Are* Our Bodies"   161

in the city. When Reich holds up the ideal of revolutionizing society in order to restore man to his roots in nature, he shows no appreciation for what man has become in his interaction with the world and for his emerging potential for greater freedom. He doesn't believe that man makes civilization to further humanize himself.

Keen: I would like to try to translate this theory into practice. How does the evolutionary vision influence the way you do therapeutic work?

Keleman: I don't look at aggression in such traditional terms as Reich or Lowen. I don't make the assumption that there is any one right way to reach out to the world, nor any single correct pattern for sexual expression. In a primitive culture if a man couldn't be aggressive, kill and rape a little, he wouldn't survive. But that has all changed. Civilization has allowed some of us to become artists and poets, to assert our existence in very soft ways. This means that the effort to construct an ideal male or female body is only a hidden orthodoxy. This is why I disapprove of the single postural ideal set up by the Alexander method or Ida Rolf's work. If we say that the male pelvis must thrust forward in a penetrating manner or it will be lacking in masculine aggressiveness and sexual pleasure, we have a new kind of chauvinism. This does not respect the individual differences in body types and life-styles. When I look at a person I ask, "How do you want to be alive in this world and what kinds of demands were made on you that prohibit you from being the person you want to be?"

Keen: Does that mean you do away with all concepts of masculinity and femininity?

Keleman: I am more interested in how a given person chooses to express his sexuality. If a man comes to me and tells me he likes to make love in a particular way with soft pelvic movements but that he doesn't feel masculine enough, I ask him what he means by not feeling masculine enough. "Well, I don't thrust hard enough; I am not aggressive; I don't get on the top enough; I don't dominate the woman."

I say all that is completely crazy, it is based on some stereotyped ideal of masculinity.

Let me put this in another way. Nowhere in Reich or Lowen is provision made for what Jung called the introverted personality. Some people choose to let the world come to them and are not terribly aggressive. Their sexual style reflects this choice. What's the matter with that?

People are so different. Some bodies are Gothic in appearance, others look like Rembrandt or El Greco paintings. I take these differences seriously. Some people make sharp, analytical penetrating movements in the world; their energy works in sharp spurts and then retracts. Others make soft and sustained contact and their energy is patterned like waves that rise and fall slowly. Some individuals need very sharp boundaries and others are softer and more diffuse.

Keen: How does therapy help a person gain individuality and freedom?

Keleman: There are two major components of good therapy. First a person must experience the way his character armor both inhibits and expresses his individuality. Character armor is body-karma, the distorted way the self has chosen to maintain itself in the world. If, for instance, a person has so tightened the abdomen that he or she has limited sexual feeling, then that very process preserves the integrity of the organism. Saying no to the self may be the only way, at times, of saying yes. By not surrendering myself, I retain control over my life. The pain and tension of chronic muscular contractions must be experienced with the knowledge that the defense systems of the psyche and the body were functional and necessary in childhood. They are expressions of the organism's chosen way of being. But blocks are not overcome merely by experiencing them and gaining insight into their origins. A person begins to experience the world in a different way. When the character armor begins to break up, vibrations, pulsations, and streaming sensations bring new awareness of life into previously deadened areas of the body. That is exciting but also scary. It takes time to be able to tolerate greater aliveness.

Keen: But don't we need something more than self-knowledge and a sampling of new sensations?

Keleman: Absolutely. There has always been a taboo against self-knowledge—don't eat of the fruit of the tree of the knowledge of good and evil. Traditional therapy tried to overcome this taboo by following the advice of Socrates: "Know thyself." But they didn't dare to break the deeper taboo: be thyself. Self-knowledge allows us to observe our biological organism from a safe distance but action requires us to commit ourselves to going beyond the known. If you want to know yourself you need to sit still, but if you want to be yourself you have to move.

Keen: If self-knowledge ends in enlightenment then action must involve endarkenment. We have so idealized the quest for knowledge and power in Western culture that we find it hard to admit that being human involves a continual groping in the darkness. We have been programed to search for light and clarity and we can't understand why our understanding doesn't make us at home in the world.

Keleman: One of the major elements in therapy is to help a person develop ways for dealing with the abiding helplessness of the human condition. I believe the fundamental truth about all neurosis is that it is a state of being helpless about helplessness. Since we are organisms in process we always face unknown situations in which we literally don't know what to do. A child knows it must escape from an emotionally intolerable situation. It doesn't know how. In therapy, a person may find it difficult to feel the energy and new sensations that are freed when old programed behaviors are broken, because he doesn't know what to do with them. Learning to deal with helplessness is a process that involves accepting the help of other people. In a relationship, a therapist shares his own sense of universal helplessness and his commitment to exploring ways to overcome it. When I work with a person I hope to give him back his own perception of his situation and the ability to use his organism in a freer way. I want to help him find a self-referring basis for his identity in his body so he can diminish his helplessness. But good therapy always brings a person face to face with the unknown and the necessity to innovate behavior. It is one thing to allow spontaneous behavior to emerge but it is another thing to take possession of it and develop it. Life is very fruitful: it gives the spontaneous and then says, "Now you develop it." It plants the seeds but we have to be the gardeners.

Keen: How would you state the goals of bioenergetics?

Keleman: I define my goal as embodiment or self-formation. *Every* organism goes through certain stages. *Life* goes from a state of universal oneness, to a state of expansion, to a state of setting up boundaries to contain energy, to a state where the boundaries are broken and the life energy goes back into the universal pool. This is death, symbolic or real. Our self-knowledge forms boundaries which contain our energy and give us definition, but when we act, or the world acts on us, we break down our boundaries and expand our sphere of being. Until actual death, we are always breaking and reforming our boundaries. I want a person to develop a sense of identification with all aspects of his biological processes: feeling, sensing, thinking, and acting. Both containment and expression, tension and relaxation are necessary for an organism to be flexible, graceful, and in contact with itself. I think that therapies like the Primal Scream are too limited in their view. Increase in the ability to feel is a good compensation for an over-development of the mind, but thought and action are important aspects of the healthy organism.

Keen: Your ideal person must be very flexible.

Keleman: And a little bit hungry as well. So long as we are alive we can expect to be incomplete and unstable. We have to give up the illusion of getting there. There is a line from one of the books of the Hebrew Haftorah I like: "And Man is a promise, he is not yet." We are open-ended organisms and so we can never reach a state of stasis.

Keen: I think religions and therapies might be defined by the way they answer the question: What are we to do about the yearning, the emptiness, the hunger, the nothingness that huddle close to the core of human experience? The Buddha's great discovery was that desire is the root of misery and eradication of desire was the way to happiness or nirvana. Augustine thought insatiable desire—concupiscence —could be quieted if it found its true object: God. Existential therapists separate neurotic and ontological anxiety and believe only some will-to-meaning will alleviate the latter. Probably the most popular way at the moment to deal with the embarrassing awareness of the incompleteness of life is with Jack Daniels, pot, or, failing that, with Librium. I think we create the problem when we define the nostalgia for completeness as abnormal or wrong. We are ashamed of our metaphysical hungers.

Keleman: Dissatisfaction is a structural component of a living organism. One of the laws of energetic functioning is that every satisfaction guarantees dissatisfaction. Every deep contact demands more contact; the more a person is able to experience and possess, the more he wants. When, for instance, a man and a woman get married and begin to satisfy their basic needs, a new demand emerges for more contact, more life, more interaction, more sociality. And that is where the trouble starts. Everytime I successfully make contact and satisfy a part of myself I create the seeds of my own dissatisfaction, because I have extended my boundaries and it is possible for me to be and experience more.

Keen: Sanity must lie somewhere in the delicate balance between our need to contain our energies within self-chosen boundaries and our need to express ourselves beyond the limits of our knowledge and security. How do you define mature sexuality? What mix of containment and expansive expression seems to create the maximum sexual satisfaction?

Keleman: I think sexuality is always on a continuum of development. What is healthy depends on where a person is in his life process. Some people can have sex galore and still not be able to integrate their sexuality with their loving or the rest of their life. Mature sexuality means being in harmony with your sexual expression and needs for your particular phase of life and knowing that this will change.

Keen: Do you think the "sexual revolution" has moved us any closer to sexual maturity? Or does it represent a new repressive orthodoxy that defines freedom in terms of the frequency and variety of sexual episodes?

Keleman: Like most revolutions it was necessary and excessive. It destroyed the unlivable ideal that there was only one right way to make love (in the missionary position in a monogamous marriage). And it provided an opportunity for people to try anything, to act out their desires, to rebel against the sexual ideals and patterns of their parents. And why shouldn't people do anything they want from monogamy to having two hundred lovers? But I don't think every form of sexual conduct can be called mature. As a person moves toward maturity, sexual excitation becomes secondary. It is the deepened feelings that become the determining factor of sexual life. And for feeling to develop there must be some containment of sexual excitation. My experience tells me that unless I care for somebody in a relationship with a lot of continuity, I will not be deeply satisfied. The ability to stay with my feelings, and not see them as something to be purged, creates a sense of anticipation, a hunger for the richest fulfillment possible. Denial and containment is itself a pleasure when it means my feelings are deepening. Even Charles Lamb understood "the ecstasy of modesty." I believe in the care and nurture of excitation, in allowing it to ripen into mature feelings.

Keen: The strong moralism and romanticism connected with sex have also created the opposite kind of problem. Some people feel deeply, contain their excitement, love, but can't express themselves sexually. Getting sexuality and tenderness together is no simple matter. Do you have different therapeutic techniques for the overexpressers and the overcontainers?

Keleman: If a person compulsively acts whenever he feels excitation, I get him to slow down his movements. Don't move the pelvis. Don't act. Breathe deeply and let the excitation build up and mellow into feelings. As feelings begin to develop, the anxiety arises and with it painful and the ecstatic memories of childhood. As this anxiety is faced, a person learns to tolerate more feelings of warmth.

If a person is capable of deep feeling but is inhibited in sexual expression, I ask him to begin to make sexual movements with the pelvis. I encourage movement, expression, action, assertion. Or I may encourage tolerance for tender feelings and gentle reaching movements. When excitation develops, we deal with the anxieties that prohibit the fusion of sex and love.

Keen: Your view of maturity, sexual and otherwise, seems to require a person to be able both to control and surrender the self.

Keleman: I don't buy the rhetoric that came out of the sensory awakening movement or out of Gestalt therapy that we have to "lose our minds and come to our senses." This view is based on the myth of innocence: all we have to do is become passive to our experience, let it all flow, merge into what is already happening. But this leaves out action. We are participants in the ongoing drama of life.

Keen: I take it you would object to the influx of Eastern spirituality which encourages us to let the ego die, give up the illusion of individuality and merge with the One.

Keleman: I think all that stuff is dangerous and misleading. Look, it is very easy to be a cosmic being, to sink into Unity. You are born a cosmic being. When you come out of your mother's womb you are in touch with universal and cosmic life. But you have very little individuality. The process of declaring or taking possession of your embodiment requires that you affirm who you are. In a sense you must turn your back on the universal if you want to claim your right as a human being. And anyone who refuses to become an individual is a shame to God or the cosmic process, because he is dealing with God's business and not his own. He denies the meaning of being born. The fact of being born is already a statement of incarnation. It involves saying no to a cosmological life, a life of polymorphous perversity, a life without boundaries or limits. One of my teachers, Karlfried Durckheim, taught me a powerful lesson: "You never kill the ego, you only find that it lives in a larger house than you thought." The authentic religious affirmation is contained in our self-affirmation.

Keen: One of the strongest motivations for the cosmic definitions of man is that it handles the fear of death by saying that only man's ego dies, while his essence is immortal. If my essence will be reincarnated, I don't need to worry about limitation, tragedy, or death. But if I am identified with this historical flesh-and-blood body that is muddling through the year 1973, it is not always easy to discover the courage to deal with my anxiety about the fragility of life and the inevitability of death. Norman O. Brown, scientologists, the Arica School, and most adherents to the growing school of transpersonal psychology deal with death in symbolic terms—the death of the ego. They don't talk much about literal death, but the grave is the reality down the road.

Keleman: If a person is an organic process, death as the termination of the process is a part of the definition of the process. We can't separate the question of the meaning of life and the meaning of death. Dying, like sexuality, is an integral expression of an organism. We choose our style of life and our style of death.

Keen: What correlations do you see between styles of sexuality and styles of dying?

Keleman: I am working on a book on death in which I deal with two types of personalities: the self-extender and the self-collector. These correspond roughly to the extravert and the introvert and could be represented by Lyndon B. Johnson and Harry S. Truman. The extender reaches out into the world and needs constant approval. He keeps pushing out and expanding and tends to be aggressive and dominant in his sexual patterns. This kind of person dies by some eruptive disease, like a heart attack. The self-collector creates very strong boundaries and allows the world to come to him. He needs little validation from other people. The collector enjoys his sensations and does not try to overwhelm. He usually dies of a degenerative disease. He dies step by step, getting hard and thin until he fades away. Often the self-extending character will facilitate his own death: the doctor says he has a heart condition and he will continue a fast pace, or when death is near he will rush toward it by suicide or just by giving up. The self-collector tries to survive inch by inch: he holds on forever out of cussedness and surrenders a little bit at a time.

Keen: Dying is complicated by our ideas about how, when and where a person may decently die. Modern medicine often deprives a person of the dignity of the final choice.

Keleman: That is because the dominant myth of our culture is that we can overcome anything. We live by the myth of the hero and so we are supposed to die bravely, alone, without protest, and without burdening other people. We are supposed to deny our deepest feelings, sacrifice ourselves for success, and neglect the pleasurable life of the body for "higher" ideals. Few people see that they have the option to create their own mythology rather than live out the cultural myth. Instead of being heroic conquerors of life, we might be explorers or experimenters or lovers.

Keen: It turns out that our myths are integrally related to the life of the body. What we may feel and experience is structured by our vision of who we are.

Keleman: The dominance of the heroic myth in our culture can be translated directly into physiological terms, into the lopsided development of one particular system. Within the human organism there is a stress system and the pleasure system. Our stress system prepares us for emergencies, for doing, for action by heightening our anxiety, shortening our breathing cycle, and creating muscular tension. The pleasure system depends largely on the opposite physiological patterns: softness, pulsation, muscular relaxation, long breathing. Our culture begins to prepare us at the moment of birth to live predominantly in stress situations. We take the child, who has been expelled from the womb and who needs contact with its mother's body to soften the shock of birth, and put it immediately into an alienated state. We move it down the hall where it can be seen and fed on schedule. That is the first stress. The breathing pattern never gets a chance to reorient itself to the pleasure state. So the child is conditioned to be dominant, competitive, fighting, and aggressive. This is the predominant neural tone of our culture.

Keen: But there is always a countercultural myth that has always been strong in America and is currently growing stronger: the myth of eternal childhood, of innocence, of the possibility of a life of perpetual pleasure. From Huck Finn to Billy Budd to the flower children to the advocates of "Consciousness Three" there is the hidden theme that America is the New Eden and we are pristine Adams and Eves. In the middle of the deteriorating environment, governmental chaos and corruption, and the dirtiest war we have ever fought, a large cadre of American intellectuals are talking about the futuristic problems of how to live in a utopia. They assume that the satisfaction of our needs will be guaranteed by a centralized government and the largest local problem will be how to deal with the threat of excess leisure.

Keleman: This reaction has come out of the exaggerated emphasis on the hero myth and the stress patterns it has created. Many people in our culture today are looking for ways to break the stress syndrome and to live in a more relaxed and pleasurable manner. This is what motivates most people to go into therapy and also explains the appeal of the new spiritual groups like Arica, and Transcendental Meditation.

Keen: Your emphasis on the pleasure system, on being grounded, on embodiment within a chosen style of life seems to have a mystical element in it, but it is concerned with the descent into the flesh rather than transcending the limits of the body. It is more related to D. H. Lawrence than Plotinus.

Keleman: When we learn to tolerate more pleasure, the world appears different from the way it looked when we were in a stressful condition. It is more open and friendly. Time changes and the analytical mode recedes, and the intuitive and receptive modes dominate. All of a sudden the world has spaces in it. It's not completely structured like the world of a paranoid. There's room for surprise, novelty, delight. It becomes viewable on a multiplicity of levels and there is sequential time and eventful time.

Keen: Do you foresee a time when there will be an authentic politics of the body?

Keleman: Currently the political world is set up in terms of eco-

"We Do Not *Have* Bodies, We *Are* Our Bodies"   171

nomic survival, and the life of the body is subservient to that value. We still live by the no-work, no-eat myth. If you don't discipline yourself and bear the pain of that discipline, you are not entitled to any pleasure. But in fact we are past the tooth-and-claw stage of history and we no longer need to live by an ethic of bare survival. Politics will change when the realization grows that we are in the middle of a radical change in the concept of man. In the past the central concern has been power. Power meant survival. The man who picked up the first stick to hit another creature was exercising power. But the man who was first able to sustain the tension so he could strike at the appropriate moment had a greater power. I think this analysis applies also to sexual power. Later, power was exercised by the ability to postpone gratification, stick to the job, and control the environment.

But then the quest for power began to alienate man. It was this insight of Marx's that captured Reich's attention. He understood that the obsession with power leads to exploitation and to cutting man off from his own sources of pleasure. Economic and sexual exploitation go hand in hand.

Keen: Looking backward, the explosion of the New Left in the sixties was motivated by the desire for a more erotic body politic. But it lacked sustaining power. It was excitation without appropriate containment.

Keleman: I think the new politics will emerge when governments have to deliver pleasure instead of power. New Left politics failed because the radicals did not respect the body. Their acid, their communes, their sexual lives were disrespectful to the life of the body.

Keen: Whatever happened to that revolution?

Keleman: It has gone back to the land to find its body, to health foods and body therapies and relationships with more commitment. The old polarity was between rigid discipline and hedonistic chaos. But these are alternatives we face. Now the question is how to create a life which is satisfying for the whole organism and how to shape politics to fit this need for wholeness.

Keen: Perhaps the new politics, like some of the new therapies, will emerge out of the effort to maximize pleasure rather than to maximize conflict.

Keleman: The change is coming even in the natural sciences. A friend of mine at the Salk Institute tells me that there will soon be a physics based on biology rather than a biology based on physics. We are coming to a time when the perception of ourselves as living creatures will determine the nature of our investigation into the universe as well as our politics. We will no longer try to see ourselves as objects in a world of objects. I think these changes will gradually bring about a new political structure based on a more holistic vision of human need.

Keen: Perhaps if we live long enough we may see some presidential candidate run on the platform "all pleasure to the people."

The Heroics of Everyday Life

A CONVERSATION WITH ERNEST BECKER

Photo: The New York *Times*

For a brief time the spotlight focused on Ernest Becker and then, for some fickle reason, it dimmed and he receded into undeserved obscurity. From 1965 to 1967 Becker was *the* professor at Berkeley. During a time of political high jinx and revolutionary sentiments he was an academic superstar to a generation of students who listened only to men whose ideas were infused with passion. As a visiting lecturer in sociology and anthropology he played to overflow audiences. With conscious drama (he once lectured from the set for King Lear) he unveiled the pathology that lies hidden beneath normality. And then with a flip of the footlights, he changed the scene to show how human a thing madness can be.

Beneath the mask of personality, underneath the facade of character, lurks the fear of death and the vast terror of the world. It is little wonder that we cling to quirks and defense mechanisms. We rather bear those perversions we have than fall into the abyss of absurdity. With bold strokes Becker limned the human condition to show how heroic we must be if we would live with truth.

Becker's thinking did not follow the political style of the sixties. He did not talk revolution. But the students loved his spacious and fiery mind and his willingness to think across departmental lines. Departmental chairmen were not so delighted. To some his popularity seemed adequate evidence that he was superficial. When no department could find funds to renew Becker's contract, 2,000 students petitioned the administration demanding that he be retained. After the administration carefully explained that they were powerless to act in departmental matters, the Berkeley student government took the matter into its hands and voted $13,000 of student-body funds to retain Becker as a visiting scholar.

Instead of accepting the students' offer, Becker traveled across the Bay to teach at San Francisco State. But the political turmoil of that school's mini-apocalypse, when Hayakawa became a household word in California, made it difficult for him to continue the careful scholarship that had always provided the foundation for his intellectual theater. In 1969 Becker, then forty-four, moved to Simon Fraser University in Vancouver, where he is professor in the department of political science, sociology, and anthropology.

His development as a generalist came about gradually. After World War II Becker lived in Europe for several years and served on the staff of the U.S. Embassy in Paris. But foreign service did not satisfy his desire to make a contribution to life. The question that obsessed him—"Why do people act the way they do?"—led him back to Syracuse University for a Ph.D. in cultural and social anthropology (1960). There he became interested in the parallels between Zen and psychoanalysis and began to develop an existential approach to psychological questions. Rather than focusing on symptoms or elaborate intrapsychic explanations for phenomena such as fetishism or paranoia, he kept asking the fundamental question: Why do we voluntarily repress ourselves and adopt crippling defense mechanisms? Becker's wide-angle vision led to an outpouring of books and articles that deal with our need to apply scientific psychological knowledge to the critical problems of personal freedom and social morality. His central concern has remained the overlap between the scientific theory of man and the theological image of him. The titles of his books reflect his persistent global focus:

Zen: A Rational Critique (Norton, 1961)
The Birth and Death of Meaning (Free Press, 1967)
The Revolution in Psychiatry (Free Press, 1967)
Beyond Alienation (Braziller, 1967)
The Structure of Evil (Braziller, 1968)
Angel in Armor (Braziller, 1969)
The Lost Science of Man (Braziller, 1971)
The Denial of Death (Free Press, 1973)

A year ago *Angel in Armor* created a wave of enthusiasm among *Psychology Today* editors and we put Becker's name on the list for a future conversation. Then in early December his new book, *The Denial of Death,* arrived and the wave swelled. On December 6th, I called his home in Vancouver to see if he would be willing to tape a conversation. His wife Marie informed me that he had just been taken to the hospital and was in the terminal stage of cancer. The next day she called to say that Ernest would very much like to do the conversation if I could get there while he still had strength and clarity. So I went to Vancouver with speed and trembling, knowing that the only thing more presumptuous than intruding into the private world of the dying would be to refuse the invitation.

Our conversation started slowly. I asked leading questions and Becker answered. At times my mind raised objections but I did not have the heart to push critical points. The hours wove us together and our talk became crisper. It was clear that Becker neither wanted nor offered intellectual quarter. The nearness of the unthinkable was not to be an excuse for thinking poorly or softening argument. As our dialogue entered what Karl Jaspers called the stage of "loving combat," the color returned to Becker's face and for two hours death was absent from the room. When it came time for me to go, we shared a paper cup of medicinal sherry the nurse had left on the night stand for Ernest. And I left, having learned something about courage that I will not forget.

Ernest Becker: You are catching me in extremis. This is a test of everything I've written about death. And I've got a chance to show how one dies. The attitude one takes. Whether one does it in a dignified, manly way; what kinds of thoughts one surrounds it with; how one accepts his death.

Sam Keen: This conversation can be what you want it to be. But I would like to relate your life to your work. And I would like to talk about the work you haven't been able to finish.

Becker: That's easy enough. As far as my work is concerned, I think its major thrust is in the direction of creating a merger of science and the religious perspective. I want to show that if you get an accurate scientific picture of the human condition, it coincides exactly with the religious understanding of human nature. This is something Paul Tillich was working on but didn't achieve because he was working from the direction of theology. The problem is to work from the direction of science. If I have anything that I can rub my hands together in glee about in the quiet hours and say, "Tee hee, this is what I've pulled off," I think I have delivered the science of man over to a merger with theology.

Keen: How have you done this?

Becker: By showing that psychology destroys our illusions of autonomy and hence raises the question of the true power source for human life. Freud, Wilhelm Reich, and particularly Otto Rank, demonstrate how we build character and culture in order to shield ourselves from the devastating awareness of our underlying helplessness and the terror of our inevitable death. Each of us constructs a personality, a style of life or, as Reich said, a character armor in a vain effort to deny the fundamental fact of our animality. We don't want to admit that we stand alone. So we identify with a more powerful person, a cause, a flag, or the size of our bank account. And this picture of the human condition coincides with what theology has traditionally said: man is a creature whose nature is to try to deny his creatureliness.

Keen: And when the half-gods go, the gods arrive? When we abandon our pseudocontrol we discover that we are lived by powers over which we have no control? Schleiermacher, the nineteenth-century theologian, said the human condition was characterized by absolute dependency, or contingency.

Becker: Exactly. I also see my work as an extension of the Frankfurt school of sociology, and especially of the work of Max Horkheimer. Horkheimer says man is a willful creature who is abandoned on the planet; he calls for mankind to form itself into communities of the abandoned. That is a beautiful idea and one that I wanted to develop in order to show the implications of the scientific view of creatureliness.

Keen: What are the implications?

Becker: This gets us into the whole problem of evil. One of the things I won't be able to finish, unfortunately, is a book on the nature of evil. I wrote a book called *The Structure of Evil,* but I didn't talk much about evil there. When I got sick, I was working on a book in which I try to show that all humanly caused evil is based on man's attempt to deny his creatureliness, to overcome his insignificance. All the missiles, all the bombs, all human edifices, are attempts to defy eternity by proclaiming that one is not a creature, that one is something special.

Searching out a scapegoat comes from the same need to be special. As Arthur Miller said, "everybody need his Jew." We each need a Jew or a nigger, someone to kick to give us a feeling of specialness. We want an enemy to degrade, someone we can humiliate to raise us above the status of creatures. And I think this is an immense datum, the idea of the dynamic of evil as due fundamentally to the denial of creatureliness. Obviously, the idea is that if you accept creatureliness you no longer have to protest that you are something special.

Keen: But in your writing you stress the need to believe that we are special. You say that we must all be heroes in order to be human.

Becker: That is true. But the important question is how we are to be heroes. Man is an animal that has to do something about his ephemerality. He wants to overcome and be able to say, "You see, I've made a contribution to life. I've advanced life, I've beaten death, I've made the world pure." But this creates an illusion. Otto Rank put it very beautifully when he said that the dynamic of evil is the attempt to make the world other than it is, to make it what it cannot be, a place free from accident, a place free from impurity, a place free from death.

The popularity of cults like Nazism stems from the need for a heroic role. People never thrive as well as when they feel they are bringing purity and goodness into the world and overcoming limitation and accident.

Keen: Do you think any of the present political crisis is due to our lack of heroic ideals? Whatever the reality of the Kennedy Administration, it did produce a sense of Camelot and a new heroic image. Nixon has given us lackluster and short-haired plumbers.

Becker: Well, America is very much looking for heroes, isn't it? I think one of the tragedies of this country is that it hasn't been able to express heroics. The last heroic war was World War II. There we were fighting evil and death. But Vietnam was clearly not a fight against evil. It is a terrible problem and I don't pretend to solve it. How does one live a heroic life?

Society has to contrive some way to allow its citizens to feel heroic. This is one of the great challenges of the twentieth century. Sometimes there is a glimpse of constructive heroics—the CCC in the mid-thirties, the camaraderie in a just war, the civil-rights campaigns. Those people felt that they were bringing a certain amount of purity and justice into the world. But how do you get people to feel that society is set up on a heroic order without grinding up some other society, or finding scapegoats the way the Nazis did?

Keen: In the terms of your understanding of society, it seems to be a Catch-22 problem. If the mass of people are encapsulated in character armor that prevents them from facing the horror of existence and therefore seeing the necessity for a heroic life, then the mass heroic models must be, by definition, unconscious. Isn't the idea of heroism an elite idea? In *The Hero With a Thousand Faces* Joseph Campbell says the hero's journey is not taken by every man.

Becker: I am using the idea of heroism in a broader sense. To be a hero means to leave behind something that heightens life and testifies to the worthwhileness of existence. Making a beautiful cabinet can be heroic. Or for the average man, I think being a provider is heroic enough. In stories and plays they make fun of the old folks when they said, "Well, I've always provided for you. I've always fed you." But those are the heroics of the average man. It is not something that one should disparage. I suppose (I haven't thought about it) that the American heroism is that one has always made a good living, been a good breadwinner, and stayed off welfare roles.

Keen: The hero as self-sufficient man.

Becker: Yes. But I don't think one can be a hero in any really elevating sense without some transcendental referent, like being a hero for God, or for the creative powers of the universe. The most exalted type of heroism involves feelings that one has lived to some purpose that transcends one. This is why religion gives the individual the validation that nothing else gives him.

Keen: I remember Hannah Arendt's lovely statement that the Greek polis was formed by the warriors who came back from the Trojan wars. They needed a place to tell their stories, because it was only in the story that they achieved immortality. Democracy was created to make the world safe for telling stories.

Becker: In primitive cultures the tribe was a heroic unit because its members and the ancestral spirits were an audience. The tribe secured and multiplied life and addressed itself to the dead ancestors and said, "You see how good we're doing. We are observing the shrines and we are giving you food." Among some Plains Indians, each person had a guardian spirit, a personal divine referent that helped him to be a hero on earth. I think this accounts for a good deal of the nobility and a dignity in some of those Indian faces we see in photographs. They had a sense that they were contributing to cosmic life.

Keen: It may be much harder for modern man to be a hero. In tribal cultures, heroism had to do with repeating archetypical patterns, following in the footsteps of the original heroes. The hero was not supposed to do anything new. We have thrown away the past and disowned traditional models. So the terror of the modern hero is that he has to do something new, something that has never been done before. We are justified only by novelty. I think this is why modern man (and with women's liberation, modern woman) is anxious and continually dissatisfied. We are always trying to establish our uniqueness.

Becker: Yeah, that's very true. Tillich concluded that for modern man to be heroic, he has to take nonbeing into himself in the form of absurdity and negate it.

Keen: In Buddhism and Eastern philosophy there is an even greater fascination with embracing the Void. The hero is the one who can overcome the desire to exist and embrace nonbeing.

Becker: I have a feeling there is a certain cleverness in Buddhism. Since you can't have what you want in the world you renounce it altogether, since you can't beat death, you embrace it. They keep talking about getting off the wheel of karma but with tongue in cheek, hoping they will get on again. Buddhism never appealed to me because it lacks an explanation of why we're here. Western man is interested in whys, and causes.

Here we are all eggs, placental eggs. We all hatched on this planet and our main life's task becomes to deny that we're eggs. We want to protest that we're here for some higher reason and we've been trying to find out what this reason is. There's no answer but the reason must be there. And it seems to me Buddhism never tries to answer these questions: Why are we here? Why do eggs hatch on this planet in the form of embryos? This seems to me our major question, the one that torments us all.

Keen: You will need to tell me when you are becoming tired because I can come and go as your energy permits.

Becker: Well, I don't know what course my illness is going to take, so I would just as soon get the conversation finished. This fatigue is not going to hurt me terribly.

I would like to talk about some of the misgivings I have about my earlier work. One of the big defects with my early work is that I tried to accommodate ideas to the opportunities of the sixties, to be relevant. Recently I have tried to present an empirical picture of man irrespective of what we need or want. Today I hold, with the Frankfurt school, that the only honest praxis is theory. There is nothing honest for the intellectual to do today in the world mess except to elaborate his picture of what it means to be a man. Man is the animal that holds up a mirror to himself. If he does this in an entirely honest way, it is a great achievement. To just run, to be driven without elaborating an image, without showing oneself what one is; this makes a creature very uninteresting.

Keen: Perhaps. But Hegel made just the opposite point: it is in blindness rather than self-knowledge that man serves the purposes of the Absolute Spirit. The cunning of the Spirit is that it uses the partial passions of man to serve the ends of the cosmos. And somehow our self-ignorance is necessary to the whole drama.

Becker: I think Hegel may be right after all. We are here to use ourselves up, to burn ourselves out. But it is still the job of the thinker is not to be blindly driven and to try to hold up a mirror for man. It doesn't follow that everyone should be in the business of trying to figure things out. In his study of primitive man, Paul Radin makes the distinction between the thinker and the man of action. The shaman is a thinker and everybody knows he is an oddball, and not a model for other members of the tribe. But the thinker of today imagines that it is the task of everybody to gain insight and be self-realized.

Keen: So the task of going beyond character is a very limited human vocation and the ordinary man must live a heroic life within the limits of his character armor?

Becker: Yes. Very few people can live without repression, without limitations. Knowing how difficult self-awareness is and what a hazardous and anxious thing it is to get rid of character armor, I would not recommend it for all people. Fritz Perls said "to die and be reborn is not easy." That is the understatement of the year. I can't imagine what many of the everyday people I know would do without their character armor. For most people mental health is a controlled obsession, the channeling of one's energies in a limited and definite direction. Those people who are self-realized still live in a very obsessed way, don't they? They have to write another book, do another job, grow, improve. They are really not very attractive creatures. They are different from the average man only in knowing that they are obsessed. I mean, here is the proof of that: I am lying in a hospital bed dying and I am putting everything I have got into this interview, as though it were really important, right? And I consider myself to be a self-realized person in the sense of having seen through my Oedipus complex and broken my character armor. But if I am going to live as a creature, I have to focus my energies in a driven way.

Keen: Is it accidental that you became fascinated with the question of death and wrote *The Denial of Death* and then became ill? Was the fascination a kind of premonition?

Becker: No. That book was finished a full year before I became sick. I came upon the idea of the denial of death strictly from the logical imperatives of all my other work. I discovered that this was the idea that tied up the whole thing. It was primarily my discovery of the work of Otto Rank that showed me that the fear of life and the fear of death are the mainsprings of human activity.

Hi Nurse, am I still alive?

Nurse: You're still alive.

Becker: This girl takes such excellent care of me. Such excellent care. It's amazing.

Nurse: Anything you need?

Becker: I would like some ice to suck on.

Nurse: OK.

Keen: Sometime I want to push you on some critical points. Is your energy high enough now, or should I wait until this afternoon?

Becker: My energy is good. My mother [the intravenous glucose] is working well.

Keen: OK. Here goes. It seems to me you do an excellent job in reviving the lost realism of the tragic vision of life, but I find a certain distortion in your perspective. Rudolph Otto said that if we look at the holy—life in the raw—it can be characterized by three ideas. It is a mystery; it is terrifying or awesome; it is fascinating and desirable. You seem to overstress the terror of life and undervalue the appeal. Life, like sexuality, is both dreadful and desirable.

Becker: Well, all right. I think that is very well put, and I have no argument with it except to say that when one is doing a work, one is always in some way trying to counter prevailing trends. My work has a certain iconoclastic bias. If I stress the terror, it is only because I am talking to the cheerful robots. I think the world is full of too many cheerful robots who talk only about joy and the good things. I have considered it my task to talk about the terror. There is evil in the world. After the reports that came out of Nuremburg about the things that were done in the death camps, it is no longer possible to have a naturally optimistic view of the world. One of the reasons we are on the planet is to be slaughtered. And tragedy strikes so suddenly. We must recognize this even as we shield ourselves against the knowledge. All of our character armor is to shield us from the knowledge of the suddenness with which terror can strike. People are really fragile and insecure. This is the truth. There is a beautiful line from *The Pawnbroker* where the main character says, "I couldn't do anything. I couldn't do anything." We do anything to keep ourselves from the knowledge that there is nothing we can do. We manufacture huge edifices of control. In Russia, for instance, they don't report disasters like plane crashes. In paradise, these things are supposed to have been eliminated.

Keen: It is like the *Christian Science Monitor*—it monitors out catastrophes.

Becker: Well, this is the control aspect of character armor which is so vital to the human being. I don't know what people would do if they had to live with the knowledge of the suddenness of catastrophe. You just can't worry that any car on the street might strike your child on the way to school. But it might. It is natural for man to be a crazy animal; he must live a crazy life because of his knowledge of death.

Keen: Another critical probe. You say man lives on two levels: he is an animal and a symbol-maker; hence he lives in one world of fact and another of illusion; and our character armor builds the illusory edifices that keep us from the threatening knowledge of the raw facts of life. But it seems to me you fall into the old positivist distinction between fact and interpretation or data and meaning. I doubt that we have anything like a raw world of facts to which we then add a layer of symbolic interpretations, Tillich always insisted, "Never say *only* a symbol." Symbolic knowledge is the highest form of knowledge we have. How can you justify the position that the *factual* world elicits only primal terror and certainty of the finality of death? The fact is we do not know. As Kierkegaard might have said, "Where do you, Ernest Becker, a historical individual, stand in order to give so certain a separation of fact and illusion?"

Becker: Yes, I see. That is a very good point. I don't really know how to answer that. What you are saying is that the symbolic transcendence of death may be just as true as the fact of death.

Keen: Right, but let me elaborate a little. Our modes of thinking about the world are basically dual. We can call them right- and left-brain dominance, or Dionysian and Apollonian, or primary- and secondary-process thinking. If we take our clues from the rationalistic, or Apollonian mode of thinking, time is linear and we are all individual atoms that end in death. But in the unconscious there are no straight lines, no time and no death.

Becker: I see what you mean. I would have to agree that the transcendence of death, symbolically or from the point of view of the whole universe, may be very real. But as a philosopher I am trying to talk to the consciousness of modern man, who by and large doesn't live in a Dionysian universe and doesn't experience much transcendence of time. I am speaking to the man who doesn't have a canopy of symbols to surround himself with and who is, therefore, quite afraid.

Keen: But our experience of being captives within time and victims of time may be more a sociological than a philosophical datum. It may reflect a judgment we should make about our society rather than about the universe. In most pretechnological cultures, death was not as much of a problem as it is today. In some cultures, death was seen as analogous to the transition from winter to spring and the resurrection of the earth.

Becker: That's right. Certain peoples believed that death was the final ritual promotion, the final rite of passage where the person became individuated to the highest degree. But we don't hold those beliefs any more.

Keen: But we have to ask ourselves why we don't. Are they intellectually invalid or have we only lost the knack of thinking with anything except the left hemispheres of our brains? One thing that is emerging from the new studies of ESP, psychokinesis, and psychic healing is that the orthodox models of mind and reality that have been considered beyond question since the nineteenth century are no longer adequate. If mind is not an isolated brain-mechanism within a machine-body, if there is something like a field or a pool of consciousnessness (the metaphors are makeshift) a hypothesis like reincarnation or the survival of consciousness becomes more interesting.

Becker: I have to admit that I am of the Apollonian bias and I can't fathom the mind of those who are into ESP and that sort of thing. I want to keep an open mind, but based on the way I see the world and feel about it, people don't communicate. People are really separate minds and separate bodies. Children and parents don't understand each other. It takes twenty years of marriage to finally communicate with one's spouse. Everyone lives in his own little compartmentalized world to an extent that is terrifying. Sam, let's put it this way: I have grown increasingly suspicious of all idealisms and all hopefulnesses. For me, it is works like Samuel Beckett's *Endgame* that give a true picture of the human condition—the terrible, hopeless, isolation of people. To me it seems like grabbing at straws to talk about left brain and right brain.

Keen: Your personal philosophy of life seems to be a Stoic form of heroism.

Becker: Yes, though I would add the qualification that I believe in God.

Keen: And to come to that point of trust you must break all illusions?

Becker: Right. The fundamental scientific, critical task is the utter elimination of all consolations that are not empirically based. We need a stark picture of the human condition without false consolations.

Keen: I prefer a more pluralistic approach. On certain days, I operate dominantly as a thinking being; on other days I am dominantly a compassionate being. And on some few lucky days I live largely in sensations. From which type of experience should I draw my clues to interpret the world? On my hard days I am a Stoic and I know that the courageous thing to do is look straight at the wintery smile on the face of truth. But on those soft days when I am permeable to everything around me, anything seems possible and I know that the courageous way is the one with greater trust and greater openness to what is strange.

Becker: I think that is good and true but it represents a level of achievement. Joy and hope and trust are things one achieves after one has been through the forlornness. They represent the upper reaches of personality development and they must be cultivated. But for people to talk of joy and happiness and to be dancing around completely under the control of their Oedipus complexes without any self-knowledge, completely reflexive, driven creatures, doesn't seem honest to me. I always watch Billy Graham because there is something spooky about this kind of reflexive joy that I can't understand. The thing has all the characteristics of straight conditioning phenomena. It is a Skinner box. And at that level I don't like to talk about faith and joy. But in the way you express it, I would want to begin talking about a higher human achievement where intellect is left behind and emotional and other types of experience start coming into play. I suppose that in my writing I have been doing an intellectual house-cleaning to make room for the higher virtues.

Keen: In the moment when your mind flips into the space where you can say, "I am a Stoic but I believe in God," what does the world look like? How do you see yourself?

Becker: Well, I suppose the most immediate thing I feel is relieved of the burden of responsibility for my own life, putting it back where it belongs, giving it back to whoever or whatever hatched me. I feel a great sense of relief and trust that eggs are not hatched in vain. Beyond accident and contingency and terror and death there is a meaning that redeems, redeems not necessarily in personal immortality or anything like that but a redemption that makes it good somehow. And that is enough.

Keen: I realize that this morning I held you at arm's length. My attitude was a perfect illustration of your thesis about the denial of death. I wanted to exile you in a category from which I was excluded —namely, the dying. That is human enough but very silly because it prevents me asking you some questions I would like to ask. As a philosopher you have thought as hard about death as anybody I know. And now, as it were, you are doing your empirical research.

Becker: It only hurts when I laugh.

Keen: And somehow, I would like to ask you what you can add now that you are closer to experience.

Becker: I see what you mean, yes. Gee, I don't know. I can't say anything that anyone else hasn't already said about dying or death. Avery Weisman and Elisabeth Kübler-Ross have been working with patients who were dying. What makes dying easier is to be able to transcend the world into some kind of religious dimension. I would say that the most important thing is to know that beyond the absurdity of one's life, beyond the human viewpoint, beyond what is happening to us, there is the fact of the tremendous creative energies of the cosmos that are using us for some purposes we don't know. To be used for divine purposes, however we may be misused, this is the thing that consoles. I think of Calvin when he says, "Lord, thou bruises me, but since it is You, it is all right." I think one does, or should try to, just hand over one's life, the meaning of it, the value of it, the end of it. This has been the most important to me. I think it is very hard for secular men to die.

Keen: Has this transcendent dimension become more tangible to you since you became ill or were you always connected through some religious tradition?

Becker: I came out of a Jewish tradition but I was an atheist for many years. I think the birth of my first child, more than anything else, was the miracle that woke me up to the idea of God, seeing something pop in from the void and seeing how magnificent it was, unexpected, and how much beyond our powers and our ken. But I don't feel more religious because I am dying. I would want to insist that my wakening to the divine had to do with the loss of character armor. For the child, the process of growing up involves a masking over of fears and anxieties by the creation of character armor. Since the child feels powerless and very vulnerable, he has to reinforce his power by plugging into another source of power. I look at it in electrical-circuit terms. Father, mother, or the cultural ideology becomes his unconscious power source. We all live by delegated powers. We are utterly dependent on other people. In personality breakdown, what is revealed to the person is that he is not his own person.

Keen: We are all possessed. Perhaps when we reach forty we begin to have the chance to expel our interiorized parents and make autonomous decisions.

Becker: Maybe. It is a fascinating phenomenon because the fundamental deception of social reality is that there are persons, independent, decision-making centers walking around. But the human animal has no strength and this inability to stand on one's own feet is one of the most tragic aspects of life. When you finally break through your character armor and discover your vulnerability, it becomes impossible to live without massive anxiety unless you find a new power source. And this is where the idea of God comes in.

Keen: But that is only one side of the story. When the personality defenses are surrendered, there is more anxiety but there is also automatically more energy, more eros, available to deal with the world since less of it is being invested in a holding action. So there is an overflow, a net increase in joy.

Becker: Yes, definitely. There is an increase in creative energies.

Keen: I would like to go on a different tack. In the days before Job, illness was thought to be the result of a divine judgment. If you were sick, it was proof that you were in a state of sin. With the introduction of the naturalistic theory of disease, suffering was severed from guilt. Now, with the advent of psychosomatic medicine, we have brought Job's comforters back to the bedside and we talk about parallels between styles of life and styles of illness. And the cruelest question that is always present, even if unasked, in the presence of illness is: "Why are you sick?" or worse yet, "Why have you done this thing to yourself?" I wonder what thoughts you have about the relation of styles of life and types of disease.

Becker: I think one of the great tragic paradoxes is that we are finding out so much about illness and psychosomatic disease and that we can't do anything about it. I go back to what I said this morning: we are driven creatures. Suppose we find out that a certain style of life leads to heart attacks or cancer. I think the approach still has to be the microscopic one, that is, the physiochemical one, because practically, people cannot change their characters. It is like the knowledge we have about how parents can induce schizophrenia in children. We know about double-binds and things like that, but we still can't envision societies taking children away from their mothers. There is no way to program society so that people aren't helplessly dependent upon other people. And this leads to depression when betrayal or abandonment occurs. So the approach must be a remedial, biochemical one, where you give people shots so they don't feel bad or at least tone down the symptomatology.

Keen: It seems to me that in some way your thought is excessively masculine—which is forgivable since you are a man. But when you talk about the effort of man to be self-sufficient, I wonder if the condition you portray is not more the masculine condition than the human condition and if it is not exaggerated by the kind of rational, competitive, masculine culture in which we live. If you were a woman how would your philosophical perspective differ?

Becker: That's some question. I don't know. Certainly heroism, the search for scapegoats, the avoidance of death, and the vain attempt to make the planet into something which it is not are as much feminine as masculine traits.

Keen: But traditionally women satisfied their immortality drive more by creating children than by fabricating artifacts. Men must create ex nihilo while women have the option of biological reproduction. I think because men's creativity inevitably involves the ephemeral world of symbols, there is greater insatiability among males than females. We make a building or write a book, and then we have to do it all over again to keep proving to ourselves that we are creative.

Becker: A book is such a shallow phenomenon compared to a child, isn't it? And it is such transient heroics compared to a baby.

I don't know about my work. I think there is an awful lot of femininity in it in terms of the kinds of things I had to feel in order to write. When it comes to the drive toward heroism, I think men are more competitive than women. The whole drama of history is the story of men seeking to affirm their specialness. One war after another has been caused by the efforts of man to make the world into something it can't be. And look at the energy we put into symbolic pursuits. You just can't imagine a feminine Bobby Fischer with that fantastic, energetic devotion to a symbolic game—chess.

Keen: If you were assigned to the job of creating a symbolic portrait of Ernest Becker to accompany this conversation, what would it look like?

Becker: If I had to do a symbolic portrait? Maybe what is significant is that I hesitate every time you ask me a personal question. My personality is very much in the background in my work. The only distinctive thing I think I have really achieved as a person is a self-analysis of an unusually deep kind.

Keen: You were never in analysis?

Becker: No, and that is a long story I had hoped at some later date to be able to write up because I think it is very important.

Keen: Then why don't you tell me about your self-analysis?

Becker: Let me say a word about this other thing first. If I were forced to paint a portrait of myself the things that come to mind are Rembrandt's successive self-portraits, in which we see him aging and see the effects of his life on his face. First, there would be the young man and every successive portrait would show the face marked by the teachings of life, by the disillusionments. It would show maturity as disillusionment into wisdom. But my first choice would be to let my ideas be presented without an accompanying portrait of me. I am very much against the cult of personality. I can't stand actors' faces or gurus' faces. I object to pushing the image of oneself as the answer to things, as the one who is going to figure things out. I have never forgotten what Socrates said. He claimed that he was obviously a better teacher than the Stoics because of his ugliness. He argued that the Stoics won people over by their handsomeness, so if a person was won over by his doctrine it had to be the doctrine itself. One ought to be won over by the force of intellectual ideas, not by the personality of the thinker. And again there is something false about a face because it implies that there is an independent person behind it, which is very rarely the case.

Keen: The self-analysis?

Becker: I think that was a big event in my life lasting over a period of years. In my mid-thirties, I suddenly started to experience great anxiety, and I wanted to find out why. So I took a pad and pencil to bed and when I would wake up in the middle of the night with a really striking dream I would write it down and write out what feeling I had at certain points in the dream. Gradually my dream messages, my unconscious, told me what was bothering me—I was living by delegated powers. My power sources were not my own and they were, in effect, defunct. I think if you are talking about analysis what you are revealing to the person is his lack of independence, his conditioning, his fears, and what his power source is. To find my way out of the

The Heroics of Everyday Life   195

dilemma my self-analysis revealed, I started exploring other dimensions of reality, theological dimensions and so on.

Keen: How has the theological perspective changed the way you view man?

Becker: Well, for instance, I was once a great admirer of Erich Fromm, but lately I believe he is too facile and too optimistic about the possibilities of freedom and the possibilities of what human life can achieve. I feel there may be an entirely different drama going on in this planet than the one we think we see. For many years I felt, like Fromm and almost everybody else, that the planet was the stage for the future apotheosis of man. I now feel that something may be happening that is utterly unrelated to our wishes, that may have nothing to do with our apotheosis or our increasing happiness. I strongly suspect that it may not be possible for mankind to achieve very much on this planet. So that throws us back to the idea of mankind as abandoned on the planet and of God as absent. And the only meaningful kind of dialogue is when man asks an absent God, "Why are we here?" I suppose, to use Tillich's terms, I am changing from the horizontal to the vertical dimension: I think a person must address himself to God rather than to the future of mankind. It would be funny, wouldn't it, if Jerusalem did win out over Athens?

Keen: The most passionate statement I heard Tillich make in the years I studied with him was that the genuinely prophetic thinkers in the modern age were those who spend a lifetime combating the Grand Inquisitor. It seems that the visions of apotheoses, of ideal states and of utopias in which there is to be no repression inevitably lead to the five-year plans and the bloodiest political purges.

Becker: The beautiful thing about America is that, whatever is wrong with us, we have not gone the road of sacrificing people to a utopian ideal.

Keen: The Greeks knew what they were doing when they said hope was the last of the plagues in Pandora's box. It seems that disillusionment must come before trust.

Becker: And the sense of joy is something achieved after much tribulation where, in the Franciscan sense, all activity stops to listen to a bird. But that is an achievement and not something that one gets in a couple of group sessions or by a few primal screams. At the very highest point of faith there is joy because one understands that it is God's world, and since everything is in His hands what right have we to be sad—the sin of sadness. But it is very hard to live that.

I think it is the task of the science of man to show us our real conditions on this planet. So long as we lie to ourselves and live in false hopes, we can't get anywhere. I don't know where we are going to get, but I think truth is a value, an ultimate value and false hope is a great snare. I always like Nikos Kazantzakis' phrase, "Hope is the rotten-thighed whore." I think the truth is something we can get to, the truth of our condition, and if we get to it, it will have some meaning. It is this passion for truth that has kept me going.

Keen: Are there other things you would like to talk about?

Becker: We seem to be all talked out, don't we? In an uncanny way we have covered everything. You have put some questions to me that really stumped me and made me think beyond what I would normally do. I am really surprised that I was able to respond to you as well as I have, because I have been very tired. But the mind works quite a bit better than the body in that sense; it has its own alertness.

I am sorry to have put you through this trial. It is a little bit like the anthropologist with the dying American Indian, you know, trying to get the last names down on the tape recorder before the Indian expires and there isn't time. You never had an interview like this before, did you?

Keen: No. But once I opened the possibility and you wanted to do it, it had to be done. And it has been an event in my life.

Becker: I am sorry I probably won't get to see it. It's funny, I have been working for fifteen years with an obsessiveness to develop these ideas, dropping one book after another into the void and carrying on with some kind of confidence that the stuff was good. And just now, these last years, people are starting to take an interest in my work.

Sitting here talking to you like this makes me very wistful that I won't be around to see these things. It is the creature who wants more experience, another ten years, another five, another four, another three. I think, gee, all these things going on and I won't be a part of it. I am not saying I won't see them, that there aren't other dimensions in existence but at least I will be out of this game and it makes me feel very wistful.

Keen: I hope I will feel that way too. I think the only thing worse would be not to feel wistful. So many people are finished before they die, they desire nothing more: they are empty.

Becker: That's a good point.

Keen: I know that what I fear more than anything is not having the green edge there until the end.

Becker: Well, if you are really a live person, I don't see how that is possible. You are bound to be more and more interested in experience. There is always more to discover.

Keen: I guess I should go.

Becker: What time is it?

Keen: A quarter after six.

Ernest Becker died March 7, 10:45 A.M.

His book *The Denial of Death* was awarded the Pulitzer Prize for General Non-Fiction (*The New Times,* May 7, 1974).

The Synthetic Vision

A CONVERSATION WITH ROBERTO ASSAGIOLI

More than half a century ago, when Freud was creating psychoanalysis in Vienna, Roberto Assagioli, M.D., was developing psychosynthesis in Italy. Until recently his work was not much known either in or outside Italy, but in the last decade institutes of psychosynthesis have been blossoming around the world and Assagioli's books are being translated into many languages.

Estimates of his accomplishment vary widely: some believe he has returned the fact of will to psychology, elaborated a viable notion of the transpersonal self, and assembled a therapeutic technology that reflects the best wisdom modern psychology can offer. Mike Murphy and Stuart Miller of Esalen think psychosynthesis provides a comprehensive vision that is likely to effect a marriage between humanistic, transpersonal, and research-based psychology. Others see Assagioli's idea of will as a Victorian throwback, his transpersonal self as a thinly disguised borrowing from idealistic theology and his techniques as an eclectic mishmash.

A Miasma of Moderation. On first reading I found *Psychosynthesis* and *The Act of Will* inclusive, ponderous and soporific. Assagioli's analyses were so balanced, his diagrams so inclusive and his solutions so global that everything bogged down in a miasma of moderation. Aristotle's golden mean may produce a mellow life, but it makes for undramatic prose. The vision of "a complete and harmonious development of the human personality" and the "elimination of all conflicts and obstacles that might block this development" seemed optimistic at best and naive at worst.

And what do you make of a psychotherapist who borrows the

best insights and techniques from a dozen competing varieties of psychology? On the American therapeutic scene we are accustomed to psychological warfare, regular shootouts at the "you're not OK" corral between members of the American Psychological Association and the Association for Humanistic Psychology. (Is it all right to touch? Is shock therapy more humane than sleeping with a client?) Balance and harmony seemed tepid fare compared to primal screams, M&Ms, and free ($$) association. I wondered what an aristocratic gentleman with a spirit of conciliation could say to us aggressive ones. Psychosynthesis did sound grand and methodical but a little too heroic. Shouldn't psychotherapy be more modest? It might be better to avoid grand visions and concentrate on the glory of coping. I had my doubts about psychosynthesis. But the alternatives are even less promising.

An Invisible Glory. A few weeks and a transcontinental flight later, I found it hard to remain critical and objective. The Renaissance oozes from every inch of Florence that is not covered by Fiats and tourists. Michelangelo's *David* testifies to the classical vision of proportion. Botticelli's *Venus* is still rising from the sea with almond-shaped, olive eyes not unlike those of a salesgirl in a small shop on the Ponte Vecchio. Il Duomo stands as a monument to an invisible glory that was once at the heart of the city. Before I entered the Institute for Psychosynthesis at 16 Via San Domenico, I was vulnerable to any hope of a majestic psychology to support the modern spirit.

Assagioli's office is a small room in his apartment, which is above the headquarters of the Institute. Books line two of the walls: Ralph Waldo Emerson, Herman Keyserling, Abraham Maslow, and Carl Gustav Jung seem to be favorites. On the next to the bottom shelf Jonathan Livingston Seagull is perched between Rollo May and Erik Erikson. The desk is antique and covered with objects and papers (talismans of the shaman): fresh-cut flowers (like tiger lilies I knew in Tennessee); a barometer; a clock; a kitchen timer; scales; a flag of the United Nations; a star globe; two word cards—ENERGY and GOOD-WILL. The walls, once white, have now yellowed like old bones. A stuffed

Victorian love seat squats in one corner of the room.

Assagioli rises to greet me. He is old, fine-boned, and frail, but the liveliness and delight in his face make his presence vigorous. His pointed goatee and salmon-colored velvet smoking jacket lend an air of old-world authority.

Roberto Assagioli: I must ask you to write the questions that you would like to ask me because, as you know, I do not hear.

Sam Keen: *(This is going to be a strange conversation. I will have to carry on two separate dialogues: one with the tape recorder and one with Assagioli. In order to keep track of his answers I will have to read my written questions onto the tape. I will also have to record my elaborations, metaquestions, doubts and occasional voices. It will be hard to capture nuances because he can only respond to specific questions. But, then, most people are deaf to the metaconversation, the thoughts beyond the words. There are four parties to every dialogue. Two are silent.)*

What are the major differences between psychosynthesis and psychoanalysis?

Assagioli: We pay far more attention to the higher unconscious and to the development of the transpersonal self. In one of his letters Freud said, "I am interested only in the basement of the human being." Psychosynthesis is interested in the whole building. We try to build an elevator which will allow a person access to every level of his personality. After all, a building with only a basement is very limited. We want to open up the terrace where you can sunbathe or look at the stars. Our concern is the synthesis of all areas of the personality. That means psychosynthesis is holistic, global, and inclusive. It is not against psychoanalysis or even behavior modification but it insists that the needs for meaning, for higher values, for a spiritual life, are as real as biological or social needs. We deny that there are any isolated human problems. Take sex for example. There is no sex per se. Sex is connected with every other function. So-called sexual problems are often caused by power conflicts between two persons and can only be solved by unraveling the complex interactions between them.

Keen: The features you have mentioned so far are largely theoretical. Is your therapeutic technology any different than psychoanalysis? *(It was always a shock to the reader of the rhetoric of logotherapy and existential psychotherapy to discover that they introduced no noticeable innovations in therapeutic practice—which may mean they made no practical difference.)*

Assagioli: Psychosynthesis makes use of more exercises and techniques than it is possible to list here. We have systematic exercises for developing every function of the personality. Initially we explore all the conscious and unconscious aspects of the personality by having patients write autobiographies, keep a diary, fill out questionnaires, and take all types of projective tests (TAT, free drawing, etc.) As therapy proceeds, we use relaxation, music, art, rhythmical breathing, mental concentration, visualization, creative imagination, evocative visual symbols and words, and meditation. But I want to emphasize that every individual is different and no techniques can be applied automatically.

Keen: Did psychosynthesis develop from psychoanalysis?

Assagioli: Yes. In 1910 Freud was unknown in Italy. My doctoral committee was reluctant, but they finally permitted me to do my doctoral thesis on psychoanalysis. I went to Zurich to study with Eugen Bleuler, the inventor of schizophrenia. When I returned, I practiced psychoanalysis in Italy, but I soon discovered its limitations.

Keen: What was your relationship to Freud and Jung?

Assagioli: I never met Freud personally but I corresponded with him, and he wrote to Jung, expressing the hope that I would further the cause of psychoanalysis in Italy. But I soon became a heretic. With Jung, I had a more cordial relationship. We met many times during the years and had delightful talks. Of all modern psychotherapists, Jung is the closest in theory and practice to psychosynthesis.

Keen: What are the similarities and differences?

Assagioli: In the practice of therapy we both agree in rejecting "pathologism," that is, concentration upon morbid manifestations and symptoms of a supposed psychological "disease." We regard man as a fundamentally healthy organism in which there may be a temporary malfunctioning. Nature is always trying to reestablish harmony, and within the psyche the principle of synthesis is dominant. Irreconcilable opposites do not exist. The task of therapy is to aid the individual in transforming the personality, and integrating apparent contradictions. Both Jung and myself have stressed the need for a person to develop the higher psychic functions, the spiritual dimension.

Perhaps the best way to state our differences is with a diagram of the psychic functions. Jung differentiates four functions: sensation, feeling, thought, and intuition. Psychosynthesis says that Jung's four functions do not provide for a complete description of the psychological life. Our view can be visualized in the diagram on p. 206. We hold that imagination or fantasy is a distinct function. There is also a group of functions that impel us toward action in the outside world. This group includes instincts, tendencies, impulses, desires and aspirations. And here we come to one of the central foundations of psychosynthesis: There is a fundamental difference between drives, impulses, desires and the will. In the human condition there are frequent conflicts between desire and will. And we place the will in a central position at the heart of self-consciousness or the Ego.

Keen: *(Beware—dangerous ground—whenever desire is opposed to will a tragic conflict appears that can only be solved by the intervention of the strong man. I suspect the iron hand of willpower lurks under the velvet glove of synthesis.)* Why do you place will at the center of the ego? Are you advocating a new form of voluntarism? Should we amend Descartes to read: I will, therefore I am?

Assagioli: I believe the will is the Cinderella of modern psychology. It has been relegated to the kitchen. The Victorian notion that willpower could overcome all obstacles was destroyed by Freud's discovery of unconscious motivation. But, unfortunately, this led modern psychology into a deterministic view of man as a bundle of competing forces with no center. This is contrary to every human being's direct experience of himself. At some point, perhaps in a crisis when danger

THE CENTER OF CONSCIOUSNESS AND
THE PSYCHOLOGICAL FUNCTIONS

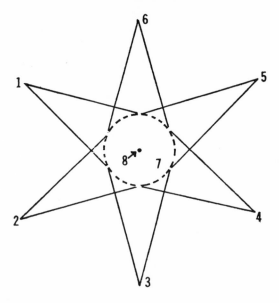

1. Sensation; 2. Emotion—Feeling; 3. Imagination; 4. Impulse—Desire;
5. Thought; 6. Intuition; 7. Will; 8. Central point. "I" or Ego.

threatens, an awakening occurs in which the individual discovers his will. This revelation that the self and the will are intimately connected can change a person's whole awareness of himself and the world. He sees that he is a living subject, an actor, endowed with the power to choose, to relate, to bring about changes in his own personality, in others, in circumstances. And this awareness leads to a feeling of wholeness, security, and joy. Because modern psychology has neglected the centrality of will, it has denied that we have a direct experience of the self. With the certainty that one has a will comes the realization of the intimate connection between the will and the

206   Voices and Visions

self. This is the existential experience of the direct awareness of pure self consciousness. It is self-consciousness that sets man apart from animals. Human beings are aware, but also know that they are aware. We can express the importance of self-consciousness, the unity of willing and being, by saying (as opposed to Descartes), "I am aware of being and willing," or, "I am a willing self."

Keen: *(I think he knocked down the deterministic house of cards which "scientific" psychology has been living in since cause and effect seized the throne. My God, he is trying to make us responsible for our identity!)*

Assagioli: I think most discussions about identity have gone wrong because academic psychologists don't take the trouble to experiment in appropriate ways. They run rats through mazes but they don't go into the inward laboratory and examine their own experience of the will. They might be compared with some irreverence to those theologians who refused to look through Galileo's telescope because they were afraid of disturbing their world view. They neglect introspection, which is the best laboratory a psychologist has.

Keen: Can you describe will further?

Assagioli: No. It is indescribable. It is a matter of direct experience, just like the direct experience of red or blue. Can you tell me what it is like to experience blue?

Keen: *(The Holy of Holies is always empty. At the heart of every system of thought lies the ineffable. Ask a rationalist how to spot a clear and distinct idea, or a Freudian how to detect an Oedipus complex, or a positivist to verify the verification principle and the answer is always a stammering that covers an embarrassed silence. The starting point is always in mystery: the subject is always that which is not exhausted by the predicates; language only leads us to the point where silence begins.)* Well, almost. Blue is cool like running water and that is very different from red which is like cinnamon or sun. When you talk of will is it something like the resolve that stiffens the Prussian backbone, or like the warm juices that run through Henri Bergson's "élan vital"?

Assagioli: No. Élan vital is, in my opinion, the true conception of libido without the specific sexual connotation given it by Freud. It is the dynamic, the power, the energy that underlies life. Will is more like the directing agent in the personality than the vital force.

Keen: But that assumes there is a single will, a single directing force. From the time of St. Paul to St. Freud the experience of the split will has bedeviled mankind. "The good I will I do not," and the will to life is in opposition to the will to death. How do you unify the conflicting wills?

Assagioli: It is certainly true that there is a multiplicity within the self, but the will is essentially the activity of the self which stands above the multiplicity. It directs, regulates, and balances the other functions of the personality in a creative way. I don't believe there is any fundamental split, any irreconcilable conflict, within man. I don't think there is a will to death opposing the will to life. What is loosely called the "split will" can be recognized to be in reality the conflict between the central will and a multitude of drives, urges, desires and wishes. This is a universal experience. Conflicts are present in every normal individual. Without them there would be no need for psychoanalysis or psychosynthesis! Each choice involves some conflict, whether to stay inside and read or go out for a walk—you can't do them both at once. In neurotic conflict there is a desperate attempt to have two incompatible things at the same time. But in the normal person the will can function to lessen or to eliminate the conflict by recognizing a hierarchy of needs and arranging for an appropriate satisfaction of all needs. The central will distributes the tasks to other parts of the personality. Let me use an analogy that is central to my thinking: the will is like the conductor of an orchestra. He is not self-assertive but is rather the humble servant of the composer and of the score.

Keen: *(I hear feminine voices in the wings: "Philosophy and psychology in the West have always been rarified forms of man-talk, usually complete with after-dinner cigars and hidden chauvinism. What of the feminine perspective? Is he describing the condition of the male psyche or of the human psyche?")* Doesn't placing the will at the center of the self betray a distinctively masculine perspective? In traditional terms, direction, control, assertion, and aggression are considered masculine attributes. The female of the species is supposedly the more welcoming, nurturing, and flowing. Do you recognize an essential "feminine" component of the self? Of the will? How do you balance the masculine and feminine elements in the self?

Assagioli: The will is not merely assertive, aggressive, and controlling. There is the accepting will, the yielding will, the dedicated will. You might say that there is a feminine polarity to the will—the willing surrender, the joyful acceptance of the other functions of the personality.

I can state the same point in another way. At the heart of the self there is both an active and a passive element, an agent and a spectator. Self-consciousness involves our being a witness—a pure, objective, loving witness—to what is happening within and without. In this sense the self is not a dynamic in itself but is a point of witness, a spectator, an observer who watches the flow. But there is another part of the inner self—the will-er or the directing agent—that actively intervenes to orchestrate the various functions and energies of the personality, to make commitments and to instigate action in the external world. So, at the center of the self there is a unity of masculine and feminine, will and love, action and observation.

Keen: *(Both/and rather than either/or. There goes the synthetic principle joining together what is usually kept apart. Eastern philosophy locates the essence of man in the atemporal observer. Western philosophy, since the rise of technology, locates the chief dignity of man in the ability to control the world, to act. Assagioli marries East and West. Do mixed marriages work, or do they produce philosophical bastards?)*

How does psychosynthesis train people to create this Olympian attitude of detached powerfulness?

Assagioli: Techniques are always related to the individual situation, so it is hard to generalize. But I can discuss two basic techniques: disidentification and training of the will.

I can begin with a fundamental psychological principle. We are dominated by everything with which our self is identified. We can dominate and control everything from which we disidentify ourselves. The normal mistake we all make is to identify ourselves with some *content* of consciousness rather than with consciousness itself. Some people get their identity from their feelings, others from their thoughts, others from their social roles. But this identification with a part of the personality destroys the freedom which comes from the experience of the pure "I."

Keen: We identify with the predicate rather than the subject.

Assagioli: That is right. Often a crisis in life deprives a person of the function or role with which he has identified: an athlete's body is maimed, a lover's beloved departs with a wandering poet, a dedicated worker must retire. Then the process of disidentification is forced on one and a solution can only come by a process of death and rebirth in which the person enters into a broader identity. But this process can occur with conscious cooperation.

The exercise in disidentification and identification involves practicing awareness and affirming: I *have* a body, but I *am not* my body. I *have* emotions, but I *am not* my emotions. I *have* a job, but I *am not* my job . . . etc. Systematic introspection can help to eliminate all partial self-identifications.

Keen: This technique is similar to the Buddhist vippissana meditation in which one merely observes passing thoughts, sensations, and images.

Assagioli: Yes, and it leads to the affirmation that the observer is different from what he observes. So the natural stage which comes after disidentification is a new identification of the self: I recognize and affirm that "I am a center of pure self-consciousness. I am a center of will, capable of ruling, directing, and using all my psychological processes and my physical body." The goal of these exercises is to learn to disidentify at any time of the day, to disassociate the self from any overpowering emotion, person, thought, or role and assume the vantage point of the detached observer.

Keen: *(Danger: the practice of disidentification may produce a per-*

son who has much light but little fire. Love is an inordinancy, therefore always blind or one-eyed. I single out one woman, one place, one work for an inordinate quantity of attention. Deep caring always involves an element of fetishism. Passion makes us lopsided. And sometimes the fastest way to the heart of things involves surrendering to forces, impulses, and desires we cannot understand, i.e., transcend. Is passion compatible with psychosynthesis? Norman O. Brown: "We are all fractions. We are broken." In the Christian tradition healing comes from accepting our brokenness not from synthesizing our parts into a perfect whole. The ideal of wholeness, realizing the full human potential, transcending contradictions, achieving enlightenment, intrigues me. But I suspect it is a secular replacement for the Kingdom of God ▸which was always coming tomorrow◂. Perhaps the human condition is inevitably colored by partialness and tragedy. Perhaps. But I owe it to myself to doubt my doubts. My resistance to the idea of life beyond conflict may be a way my ego holds on to contradiction. Would I still be me if I were happily synthesized?)

I see how you arrive at the pure experience of the self as observer, but how can you claim that the will is capable of ruling and directing all the other psychological functions? Frequently the will seems powerless to master infantile drives. At times it is a powerless prisoner governed by an infantile tyrant. When depression strikes, or anger surges, or sexual desire bubbles up, willpower seems weak, more like an aging parent than a virile manager of the personality.

Assagioli: Will, like any other function of the personality, can be systematically developed and strengthened. If it is weak it can be trained by regular exercise in the same way muscles are developed by gymnastics. And if a person begins with a weak will he may, by the simple miracle of overcompensation, develop a greater than normal strength of will. Everybody has enough will to begin the process of developing more.

Keen: *(Whenever anyone talks about developing willpower, two contradictory images rise before me. (1) The self-made man: Horatio Alger, Dale Carnegie, and How To Develop A Powerful You in 30 Days.*

I suspect superficiality. (2) The victim. Neurosis is inner passivity. Depression is learned helplessness. Without a strong will a person remains a victim. Maybe. The ambivalence about the concept of will, or rather its neglect, in modern psychology is a reflection of an embarrassment about the desire for personal power. Our power drive has been externalized and channeled into science and technology, politics and warfare. Why not have the development of inner potency as an overt goal?)

What other techniques do you use to develop willpower?

Assagioli: Let me clarify something. Psychosynthesis is not primarily concerned with developing willpower. Strength is a necessary but not a sufficient condition of the will. It is equally important to develop a skillful will and a good will. We have many techniques for developing each of these qualities. I deal with these at length in *The Act of Will.* One technique is visualizing the "ideal model." Picture as vividly as possible how your life would be different if you were in possession of a strong will. Visualize yourself as having attained inner and outer mastery. We also advise performing some "useless exercises" every day for strengthening self-discipline. You can resolve to stand on a chair for ten minutes or run a mile a day or control a violent temper. Developing a skillful will is more difficult. If the will is placed in direct opposition to strong feelings or drives, it will be overpowered and so we have to create a strategy to achieve the ends we will. Take, for example, a person with an obsessive desire who wills to be rid of his obsession. The more he concentrates on the obsession, the fiercer it grows. But he can withhold his attention and substitute a new interest; he can cultivate a beneficent "obsession." Holding new images before the eyes tends to produce the reality suggested by the image. This follows from a well-known psychological law: images or mental pictures and ideas tend to produce the physical conditions and external acts that correspond to them. Or, as William James said, "Every image has in itself a motor element." One very simple technique I use is a series of cards on which are printed evocative words such as: CALM, PATIENCE, BLISS, ENERGY, GOOD

WILL. When these cards are placed around the room, they trigger attitudes and call forth the quality they symbolize. I also use works of art in a similar way. For instance Fra Angelico's *Transfiguration* is a visible symbol for the transformation of the personality which takes place when a person gets in touch with the transpersonal Self.

Keen: *(Is this simpleminded, or a judicious use of the automatic responses of the body/mind? I am not certain. Confession: One evening I put up the card named* GLORY *in my hotel room and waited for results. In the morning I awoke in rumpled and musty sheets to streaming sunlight and church bells and a golden day filled with florentine coffee, Leonardo da Vinci, and—most certainly—glory. But we all know such attitudinal overlays are due to the power of suggestion, don't we?)*

Good will seems to belong more to religion than psychotherapy. Can't the will be healthy without being good?

Assagioli: No. A person is always in a social context; he is not an isolated unit. So the more conflict there is, the more energy is wasted. If we are to have any deep peace, it depends upon the harmonization of wills. Self-centeredness is deeply destructive to the cooperation without which a person cannot live a full life in community. Why should we consider good will an expendable virtue, a matter only for the religious? I can go even a step further. This same principle applies to an individual's relation to nature and the universe. No person can take an arrogant stand and consider himself unrelated to the universe. Like it or not, man is a part of the universal will and he must somehow tune in and willingly participate in the rhythms of universal life. The harmonization and unification of the individual and the universal will —the Chinese identification with the Tao, the Stoic acceptance of destiny, or the Christian will of God—is one of the highest human goals, even if it is seldom realized.

Keen: Until Maslow began to talk about metaneeds, psychology was embarrassed by anything that looked like metaphysics or religion. Now it seems that mysticism and medicine are joining forces. Does healthy self-awareness necessarily involve a religious commitment?

Assagioli: Not necessarily. What I call personal psychosynthesis can be achieved by coming to understand the lower and the middle unconscious. But for some people, when basic psychological needs have been met and a measure of health has been achieved, boredom and a sense of meaninglessness set in and a search begins for some higher purpose in life. As Jung pointed out, being normal and adjusted is enough for some persons, but others have a hunger for transcendence. There is a new "fourth force" in psychology—transpersonal psychology—which seeks to explore those needs and aspirations that go beyond self-actualization and humanistic psychology.

Keen: In Freud's time there was a vast cultural conspiracy to repress the libido, to force it to remain unconscious. Would you say we have a parallel conspiracy to repress the religious impulse? We seem as ashamed of our appetite for meaning as Victorian society was of erections and palpitations not of the heart.

Assagioli: Many people seem to have voluntarily submitted to a spiritual lobotomy, to a repression of the sublime, a complete denial of the transpersonal self. Consequently the higher unconscious remains virtually unknown to many people. Much psychology has encouraged the adoption of a degraded self-image by advancing the argument that all religious or spiritual impulses are mere sublimations of sexual instincts. This type of reductionism ignores the fact that many of the most creative people in human history report experiences of a transpersonal nature. By what right can we deny that spiritual drives are less real, basic, or fundamental than sexual or aggressive drives?

Keen: Why should people repress the sublime? What's so threatening about paradise?

Assagioli: It is no more mysterious than the repression of sexual ecstasy. We fear the sublime because it is unknown and because if we admit the reality of higher values we are committed to act in a more noble way. Goodness, cooperation, the loss of self-centeredness, and responsibility for spiritual growth go along with acknowledgement of the higher self.

Keen: What is the nature of the transpersonal self? Are you talking about an entity separate from the self we experience directly in self-awareness?

Assagioli: My dear friend, I cannot tell you what the transpersonal self is like. Maslow tried to characterize it and the nature of the peak experience in *The Psychology of Being.* Direct experience of the transpersonal self is rare and union with it is very rare. But many people have a knowledge of it that is mediated through the higher unconsciousness or the superconsciousness. I can describe some of the effects. It is spontaneously manifested in the creative works of the great universal geniuses such as Plato, Dante, and Einstein. Others get in touch with it through prayer or meditation. Or they may feel a call or pull from some Higher Power. Language is always inadequate to speak about transpersonal or spiritual experiences. Every expression is highly symbolic, and a large variety of symbols have been used: enlightenment, descent into the underworld of the psyche, awakening, purification, transmutation, psychospiritual alchemy, rebirth, and liberation.

Keen: I assume you have techniques in psychosynthesis to develop awareness of the transpersonal self.

Assagioli: Yes. Among them the technique of inner dialogue works well. Imagine a very wise man who knows the answers to all the problems you face. If you could obtain an interview with this man what would he tell you? This is your inner teacher . . .

Keen: *(I fear my inner guru may be senile. He seems to offer contradictory advice: take it easy/work harder, risk everything/stay where you are, dare madness/cultivate sanity. He can never decide whether he is on the side of Dionysus or Apollo.)*

Assagioli: . . . If you listen for an answer you may find it coming spontaneously through a third person or a book you are reading or through the development of circumstances. The practice of meditation also is good. Sometimes I suggest that clients write a letter.

Keen: To the transpersonal self?

Assagioli: Yes. "Dear Transpersonal Self . . ." Try it and see what happens.

Keen: To what address do I mail it?

Assagioli: To the same place you mail the angry letters you write when you tell a lover or enemy all the things you hate about him.

Keen: I can never quite decide whether psychosynthesis techniques are naive or brilliant. They frequently seem a little simpleminded to me. *(Should I admit that after yesterday's session and his "simplistic" analysis of neurosis as vacillating in the decision seat, I stopped smoking cigarettes for happily-ever-after?)* There is an old tradition that links wisdom and foolishness. Is a wise man simpleminded? Is the simplification that comes with age wisdom or fatigue? And is psychosynthesis a modern version of a wisdom school? What is the difference between a wise man and a fool?

Assagioli: Wisdom is even more out of fashion today than will. The original notion of wisdom has little to do with foolishness. Of course wisdom does involve a higher simplicity of the spirit, but this is not simplemindedness. In Chinese the ideograph for wisdom is a combination of wind and lightning. So the wise man is not the one who is serene and tired, but one who can no more be captured than the wind and who strikes like lightning when necessary. Wisdom is connected with intuition (that is why she has been seen as a woman: Sophia) and with seeing things whole, and so it links up with the transpersonal perspective. It is the power to play with opposites and to establish a synthesis. I suppose that age helps one to acquire some of the perspective necessary to create harmony among the apparent contradictions.

Keen: William Blake said, "The way of excess leads to the palace of wisdom." Shouldn't youth be a time of excess rather than striving for a premature balance?

Assagioli: That's amusing.

Keen: Here is another quote [from the Scottish philosopher McNab, I think] that goes with it: "Wisdom is a virtue in the second half of life but a bore in the first." Shouldn't psychosynthesis be reserved for those over forty?

Assagioli: You will excuse my not giving you a wholesale answer. Individuals differ. Some young people are psychologically mature and some adults are childish psychologically. Some personal psychosynthesis must take place before the transpersonal psychosynthesis, but people are ready for this at different ages.

Keen: What are the limits of psychosynthesis? If you were a critic of your own system, what would you criticize?

Assagioli: That should be your job but I will do it. It is fun. I will answer paradoxically. The limit of psychosynthesis is that it has no limits. It is too extensive, too comprehensive. Its weakness is that it accepts too much. It sees too many sides at the same time and that is a drawback.

Keen: *(That's my "self-knowledge index" question. Most "famous" people get about C—. I give Assagioli a straight A. He sees in the back of his own eyes.)*

Hannah Arendt says that forgiveness is the key to action and freedom. Without forgiveness life is governed by the repetition compulsion, by an endless cycle of resentment and retaliation. Yet few psychotherapists tip their hats to it. Some, like Janov, seem to encourage resentment and anger against parents and society because they are the source of primal pain. Tell me what psychosynthesis has to say about forgiveness, responsibility, and gratitude.

Assagioli: In psychosynthesis we stress individual responsibility. No matter what has happened to a person, he must assume responsibility here and now for changes he wants to make in his personality and not blame his parents or society. I am against many things in modern society and am a revolutionary in that sense, but we have to change it from within because it is our society. Toward those persons who have harmed you I recommend understanding and pity. Probably the harm is not so great as you imagine. Of course we are conditioned by the past but we have the power to disown it, to walk away, to change ourselves. Most of the harm parents do to children is done out of ignorance and not malice, and so it is liberating to forgive those who knew no better, rather than harbor resentment and self-pity. Also, forgiveness becomes easier when you come in contact with the real suffering of humanity. One thing I would propose in education is that young people have a weekly visit to hospitals, institutions for the insane, and slums, so they come directly into contact with human suffering without the interposition of theories, statistics, or political ideologies.

Keen: Since the decline of religion in the West and the loss of the rites of passage—birth and death rituals—it has fallen to psychology to help people cope with transition crises and boundary situations. How do you deal with death? At eighty-five, how does it appear to you?

Assagioli: Death looks to me primarily like a vacation. There are many hypotheses about death and the idea of reincarnation seems the most sensible to me. I have no direct knowledge about reincarnation but my belief puts me in good company with hundreds of millions of Eastern people, with the Buddha, and many others in the West. Death is a normal part of a biological cycle. It is my body that dies and not all of me. So I don't care much. I may die this evening but I would willingly accept a few more years in order to do the work I am interested in, which I think may be useful to others. I am, as the French say, *disponable* (available). Also humor helps, and a sense of proportion. I am one individual on a small planet in a little solar system in one of the galaxies.

Keen: *(It is hard to know what counts as evidence for the validity of a world view and the therapeutic it entails. Every form of therapy has dramatic successes and just as dramatic failures. Enter as evidence in the case for psychosynthesis an* ad hominem *argument: in speaking about death there was no change in the tone or intensity of Assagioli's voice and the light still played in his dark eyes, and his mouth was never very far from a smile.)*

Roberto Assagioli died August 23, 1974, rich and full of years.

74 75 76 77 10 9 8 7 6 5 4 3 2 1